Workbook

EARTH & SPACE SCIENCE

SCIENCE

Exploring the Universe

Dr. Gustavo Loret de Mola

Wright Group

The **McGraw·Hill** Companies

Author
Gustavo Loret de Mola, EdD

Series Consultants
Richard Audet, EdD, Roger Williams University
Matthew Marino, PhD, Washington State University
Barbara Scott, MD, Los Angeles Unified School District
Lisa Soll, BS, San Antonio Independent School District

Art Credits
Richard Carbajal

ELL Consultants
Mary Smith, MA, Merced, California
Brian Silva, MS, Long Beach, California

Laboratory Reviewer
Garrett Hall, BA, Pleasant Hill, Iowa

Laboratory Safety Consultant
Jeff Vogt, MED, West Virginia University
at Parkersburg

www.WrightGroup.com

Wright Group

Copyright © 2009 by Wright Group/McGraw-Hill

Printed in the United States of America.
Send all inquiries to:
Wright Group/McGraw-Hill
P.O. Box 812960
Chicago, IL 60681

ISBN 978-0-07-704152-6
MHID 0-07-704152-6

1 2 3 4 5 6 7 8 9 MAZ 13 12 11 10 09 08

Contents

Key Concept Review

PART A Vocabulary

Answer each question below using the correct term from the box. You will not use all of the terms.

atmosphere
biosphere
density
geography
geology
hydrosphere
lithosphere
mass
variable

1. The hard outer shell of Earth is called the _____.

2. The environments on Earth and the living things within them make up the _____.

3. The study of Earth's features is called _____.

4. A factor that can change in an experiment is called a _____.

5. The amount of matter in an object is called its _____.

PART B Comprehension

Answer each of the questions about Earth science on the lines provided.

6. How is oceanography related to the study of weather? _____

_____

_____

7. Name another branch of Earth science that geographers need to understand. Explain. _____

_____

8. What are the other names for the SI system? _____

_____

SCIENCE EXTENSION

Scientists must gather data in order to test their hypotheses, and this often involves using a measurement system. Use what you have learned about the SI system and the scientific method to write a paragraph on how you might gather data about your local weather. What makes it possible for you to compare your data with that of your local meteorologist? How would you compare it with similar weather data from past years? Can you use your data to make any predictions?

Chapter 1

Studying Earth Science

Vocabulary Review

PART A

Match each term in Column B with its description in Column A. Write the letter of the correct term in the space provided.

Column A

_____ 1. the variable that is observed for changes

_____ 2. the amount of space that an object takes up

_____ 3. it explains the scientific results of many experimental trials

_____ 4. the relationship between mass and volume of an object or substance

_____ 5. it is a possible answer to a scientific question

_____ 6. the amount of matter in an object

_____ 7. the experimental variable that is changed

Column B

a. density

b. dependent variable

c. hypothesis

d. independent variable

e. mass

f. theory

g. volume

PART B

Use one of the following terms to fill in the blanks: *geography, geology, hydrology, meteorology,* and *oceanography.* Next, fill in the diagram by writing one of the four major Earth systems and its definition in each box. In the blank next to each box, provide an example of one branch of Earth science that relates to that Earth system.

8. _____ study of Earth's features and distribution of life on Earth

9. _____ study of weather patterns in Earth's atmosphere

10. _____ study of water and how it moves on Earth

11. _____ study of solid Earth

12. _____ study of Earth's oceans

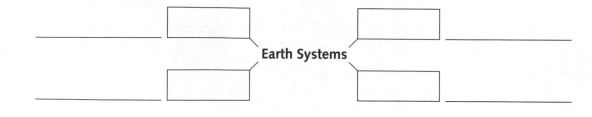

Earth Systems

SCIENCE EXTENSION

In your Science Notebook, describe a situation in which an Earth scientist is using the International System of Units (SI system) while collecting or observing data. Explain why the scientist chose to use the unit or units.

Graphic Organizer

PART A

Complete the table by describing the area of study for each branch of Earth science.
Then search the library or Internet for information, and include at least three careers.

Branches of Earth Science		
Branch	**What the Branch Studies**	**Possible Careers**
Astronomy	1.	2.
Atmospheric science	3.	4.
Oceanography	5.	6.
Hydrology	7.	8.
Geology	9.	10.
Geography	11	12.

PART B

In the space next to the description of each Earth system, write *A* for atmosphere,
B for biosphere, *H* for hydrosphere, or *L* for lithosphere.

_____ **13.** living things and the environments in which they live

_____ **14.** water in its vapor, liquid, and solid forms

_____ **15.** keeps Earth from getting too hot or too cold

_____ **16.** helps give shape to Earth's surface

SCIENCE EXTENSION

In your Science Notebook, draw a diagram that shows how an event, such as an
earthquake, tsunami, hurricane, or volcanic eruption, might affect the atmosphere,
biosphere, hydrosphere, and lithosphere.

Reading Comprehension

PART A Outlining

Outlines can help you study. Go back to Lesson 1.1 in your textbook. Look at the headings, the subheadings and vocabulary words. Write a brief summary about each heading.

I. Lesson 1.2 The Scientific Method

A. Heading

1. Ask a Question _____

2. Form a Hypothesis _____

3. Test the Hypothesis _____

4. Analyze Data _____

5. Draw Conclusions _____

6. Communicate Results _____

PART B Comprehension

Your textbook uses many terms that might be new to you. Sometimes these new terms are defined. Sometimes you have to use context clues or the dictionary to find out what they mean.

7. In your own words, define *analyze*. _____

8. What is the standard SI unit for volume? _____

9. Why might an astronomer want to study other planets and galaxies? _____

SCIENCE EXTENSION

Safety really RULES! Read each safety scenario. Then point out the safety rule or rules that were broken in each. Write your answer in your Science Notebook.

1. With her safety glasses on, Gina put the flask near her nose and sniffed.

_____

2. Patrick had a lot of a chemical left from an experiment. He dumped the chemical in the sink and turned on the water to wash it down the drain. _____

History Connections: The Smokestacks of the Industrial Revolution

PART A

The Industrial Revolution took place between 1750 and 1850. During this period, the economies in the United Kingdom and the United States changed from farming to factories. The increase in coal-fired steam engines fueled a new society. It was an era best symbolized by giant factory chimneys belching out dark, sooty smoke that could darken the day at noon. The air pollution resulted in the formation of acid rain. While the Industrial Revolution might be over, acid rain persists.

Complete the graphic organizer using the following terms: *atmosphere, biosphere, hydrosphere,* and *lithosphere.*

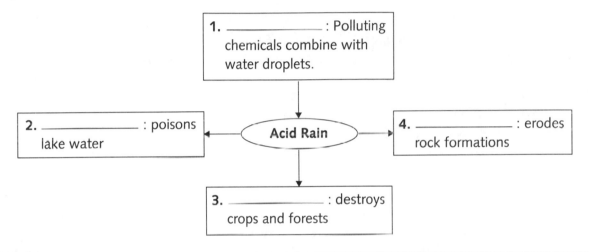

1. _____ : Polluting chemicals combine with water droplets.

2. _____ : poisons lake water

Acid Rain

4. _____ : erodes rock formations

3. _____ : destroys crops and forests

PART B

Use what you have learned to answer the questions below.

5. What does water on Earth's surface produce when it interacts with air? _____

6. What part of sunlight can cause a sunburn? _____

7. What is the study of objects and events beyond Earth's atmosphere? _____

8. What is the first step to solving a problem according to the scientific method?

_____

SCIENCE EXTENSION

Knitting Up the Ozone Hole

Ecology Connection Human activities can affect all of Earth's systems. Ten years after countries agreed to ban CFCs (chlorofluorocarbons), CFCs reached their highest levels in the atmosphere. Twenty years later, measurements show that the ozone hole shrinks and expands throughout the year, but overall is not getting any bigger. In terms of Earth's spheres, what does this tell you about ozone and ecological damage?

Challenge Activity

PART A Tools Used in Earth Science

Earth scientists use many tools. Some are used to examine small objects or distant objects, such as stars and planets. Others help locate things that are underwater, and still others are used to communicate.

Barometer Air exerts pressure on Earth's surface. A barometer is an instrument that measures this pressure.

Microscope Microscopes use lenses to magnify small objects. They are used to look at objects that are too small to be seen with the unaided eye. Microscopes can also be used to examine things, such as rocks and minerals, more closely.

Telescope Telescopes also use lenses, but these lenses gather and magnify light that comes from great distances. Telescopes are used to see distant planets and stars. A telescope may be on Earth's surface, or it might be placed into orbit around Earth.

Sonar Sonar is a tool that uses sound to locate objects underwater. A sound that is sent through water will hit underwater objects. Once the sound wave hits an object, it will bounce off, or echo back. These echoes are analyzed and used to find out how far away the object is. Scientists use sonar to measure ocean depths. It is also used by the Navy to detect underwater objects and to communicate underwater.

Artificial satellite Artificial satellites are synthetic instruments that move through space around Earth (or, sometimes, other planets). There are many different types of satellites. Some gather information about Earth. They may take pictures or measure the temperature in clouds or various surface locations. Other satellites are used for communication. Still others are used to help aircraft, ships, cars, or even individual people determine their locations on Earth.

1. Think about Earth's systems. Which system is being studied by people who use barometers?

    _____

2. Artificial satellites have been used for almost 50 years. Use the library or Internet to find out information about the very first one. What was it called? When was it sent into space? Which country sent this satellite into space? _____

    _____

    _____

    _____

    _____

3. Think about why someone (such as a scuba diver, fisher, or navigator) would want to locate something underwater. Use complete sentences to explain how you think that person might use sonar in their work.

_____

_____

_____

4. The *Hubble Telescope* is in space, orbiting around Earth. Use the library or Internet to find out more about the telescope. In your Science Notebook, write a complete paragraph about this telescope. Briefly describe its history, how long it is expected to collect data and take photos, and what types of things it has been used to observe. Also find and describe some photos taken by the telescope.

_____

_____

_____

_____

_____

_____

_____

_____

_____

PART B

Now that you have learned more about these tools, identify which of them may be used in different branches of Earth or Space science. Write these in the table below.

Branch of Earth Science	Tools Used
Atmospheric science	
Oceanography	
Geology	
Astronomy	

Key Concept Review

PART A | Outlining

As you read, fill in the outline below using the main titles and headings of each lesson in this chapter.

2.1: _____   2.2: _____

   A. _____   A. _____

   B. _____   B. _____

   C. _____   2.3: _____

   D. _____   A. _____

   E. _____   B. _____

   F. _____   C. _____

   G. _____   D. _____

PART B | Vocabulary

Circle the correct term in each sentence below.

1. A map (projection, scale, key) is a way to draw a view of a round object on a flat surface.

2. Lines of (latitude, longitude, curvature) run from the south pole to the north pole.

3. A map (projection, scale, key) tells how big or small the map is in comparison to the area that it represents.

4. (True north, Magnetic declination, The equator) is the point around which Earth rotates.

5. A (latitude, longitude, contour) line is a line on a topographic map that connects all points that have the same elevation.

SCIENCE EXTENSION

How do maps show the features of the planet on which we live? Create a map of your town, and use what you have learned in this chapter to add land features to your map. Be sure to include a north arrow on your map and use what you have learned about topographic maps to show changes in elevation. Create a map key for your map, and remember to include a map scale.

Vocabulary Review

PART A

Complete the table below.

Term	Definition	Example(s)
1.	the difference in elevation between one contour line and the next	**2.**
contour line	**3.**	**4.**
elevation	**5.**	**6.**
7.	contour lines drawn darker and thicker and are labeled with elevation	**8.**
9.	explains what the symbols used on a map represent	**10.**
topographic map	**11.**	**12.**

PART B

Match each definition to one of the terms in the list below. Write the letter of the definition in the blank next to the term.

13. _____ latitude

14. _____ magnetic declination

15. _____ Prime Meridian

16. _____ longitude

17. _____ map scale

18. _____ true north

a. the geographic pole around which Earth rotates

b. compares a map to the area it represents, given as a ratio between the two

c. angle of correction for the difference between geographic and magnetic north

d. a measurement of distance, in degrees (°), north or south of the equator

e. a reference line that passes through Greenwich, England

f. a measurement of distance, in degrees (°), east or west of the Prime Meridian

SCIENCE EXTENSION

Describe a situation in which you would need to use remote sensing, sonar, the Global Positioning System (GPS), or the geographic information system (GIS). Explain the technology and why you would use it for that situation.

_____

_____

Interpreting Diagrams

PART A

Identify the following: Mercator projection, conic projection, azimuthal projection, equator, Prime Meridian, lines of latitude, and lines of longitude.

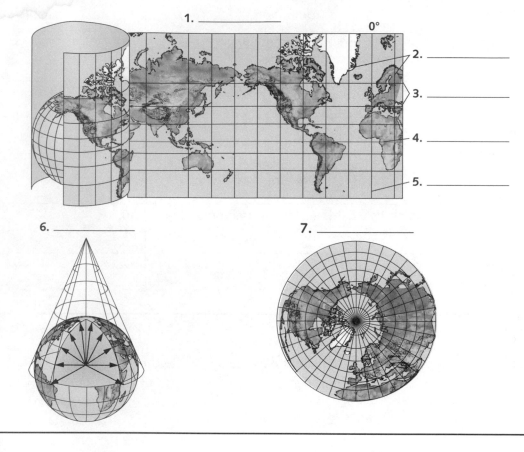

1. _____

0°

2. _____

3. _____

4. _____

5. _____

6. _____

7. _____

PART B

Write the name of the map type described in each question below.

8. shows the shortest path between two points _____

9. best projection for mapping small areas _____

10. point of projection usually north or south pole _____

11. shows cardinal directions in straight lines, so it is useful for navigating _____

12. often used to make road and weather maps _____

13. distorts size of land near the north and south poles _____

SCIENCE EXTENSION

In your Science Notebook, write a short guide on how to use a topographic map when hiking in the mountains. The guide should be easy to understand and should include illustrations where necessary.

Reading Comprehension

PART A Vocabulary Word Map

As you review Chapter 2, make a vocabulary term map in your Science Notebook for at least four vocabulary terms from each lesson. For each term, the map should include a definition in your own words, a synonym or antonym, the term used in a sentence, and a drawing to help you remember its meaning. To get you started, complete the map shown below for the word *longitude*.

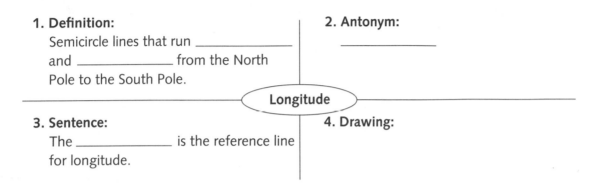

1. Definition:
Semicircle lines that run _____ and _____ from the North Pole to the South Pole.

2. Antonym:
_____

Longitude

3. Sentence:
The _____ is the reference line for longitude.

4. Drawing:

PART B Location, Location, Location!

Using a topographic map can give you a clear understanding of a location's natural and human-made features. Read each of the following scenarios. In your Science Notebook, explain how a topographic map would come in handy.

5. Claire and her friends have not exercised in a long time. They are considering different areas in their state in which to go hiking.

6. The city planners in Nan's town are looking for the best location to build an airport.

SCIENCE EXTENSION

Truth or Consequence?
Ray tries to impress his date by telling her that he is a GIS technician. For each of the following statements Ray made, help his date figure out whether he might be telling the truth about his occupation.

1. "Two things I really like are maps and working on a computer." _____

2. "I have always loved science. I took as many science classes as I could in college." _____

3. "Last week I had to produce a map for a client that showed which way a stream flows and how long it takes nutrients to travel downstream." _____

4. "You do believe me, don't you? Look, my paycheck was issued by our local city government."

_____

Technology Connections: Tools of Discovery and Exploration

PART A

Throughout history, advances in technology have led to a deeper understanding of the world around us. The invention of the sail made ocean voyages possible and opened up new trade routes connecting people and cultures. The microscope and telescope were both invented more than 400 years ago. Each led to new discoveries. Today, the remote sensing technology used in satellites and interplanetary probes is opening up a whole new world for us to explore and discover.

Complete the graphic organizer using these terms: *Landsat, Earth's surface, ocean floor, sonar,* and *sound waves.*

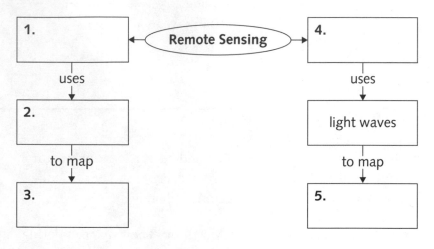

PART B **Use what you have learned.**

6. Does a Mercator projection map cause areas near Earth's poles to appear larger or smaller? Explain.

_____

7. Does a compass needle point toward the magnetic north pole or the geographic north pole? Explain.

_____

8. On a map, if a trail crosses a contour line, in which direction is it going? _____

SCIENCE EXTENSION

Maps Tell All

Technology Connection Today, anyone surfing the Internet can download maps with satellite images. The maps are highly detailed. Some show areas few people could access legally, such as nuclear energy plants or military installations. Is it right for such information to be available to everyone? Write a paragraph in your Science Notebook arguing whether or not you think access to this kind of information should be restricted or not. Be sure to support your opinion.

Chapter
2

Challenge Activity

PART A Latitude and Longitude

There are many ways to describe the location of a place. Its exact location on Earth can be given using latitude and longitude. Think about a city that you have always wanted to visit. Where is this city? In which country is it? On which continent is this country? Is it in the northern or southern hemisphere?

1. Write the name of your chosen city below. Then use a world map to describe its exact location using latitude and longitude. Remember to use minutes and seconds if necessary.

_____

_____

_____

_____

_____

2. Now imagine that you have travelled 50°W longitude. What is your new location?

_____

_____

_____

_____

_____

3. Now imagine that you have travelled 50°S latitude. Describe your new location.

_____

_____

_____

_____

_____

_____

PART B Reading Maps

4. Imagine that you are taking a trip to one of the cities above. You want to plan some events before you go. Find a current street map of the city by using guide books or the Internet and use this map to plan a two-hour afternoon walking tour. Imagine that you will be walking 1.4 miles, or 2.2 kilometers, in one hour. On a copy of your map, draw a line with arrows to show where you will walk during the two hours of your tour. Put a star at any attractions you wish to see.

5. Perhaps you are a person that enjoys the outdoors more than cities. Use books or the Internet to choose an interesting location to go hiking. Find maps of this area and plan a route to take on the map. This time imagine that you could walk two miles in one hour on low hills, and less far on mountains or steep hills. Make a list of supplies that you would take with you. Which of these supplies could help to keep you from getting lost?

_____

_____

_____

_____

_____

SCIENCE EXTENSION

Drawing Maps

Maps can be made to represent any place and describe locations of things within any place. To try your hand at mapmaking, make a map of a room in your home. First, take measurements of the room with a tape measure. Then decide on a map scale that will fit onto a small- to medium-sized piece of paper. For example, if your room is 10 feet (120 inches) long, you may wish to make a map that is 1 foot (12 inches) long. Remember to include the scale on your map.

Draw all of the objects in the room on the map and make a legend. If the room contains a hill-like shape, such as a pile of laundry, use contour lines and index contours to show its height. Finally, choose a color code for your map. For example, you may wish to make all places to sit one color and all hard surfaces, such as tabletops, a different color.

Key Concept Review

PART A Classify

Label the graphic organizer below with the three lesson titles in this chapter. Read each vocabulary term's definition, then write the vocabulary term in the appropriate box.

bond between two atoms that share electrons

two or more atoms held together by covalent bonds

number of protons in an atom

bond that holds metals together

anything that has mass and takes up space

tiny particle that is neutral

process during which one or more substances turn into new substances

bond that holds together two ions that have equal and opposite charges

mixture with visible parts

smallest unit of an element that has characteristics of that element

tiny particle with a positive electric charge

original substances

tiny particle with a negative electric charge

new substances that are a result of a reaction

Matter and Atoms

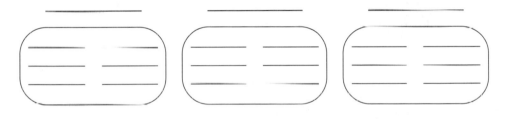

PART B Comprehension

Answer each of the questions below on the lines provided.

1. What are the three basic particles that make up an atom?

    _____

2. Do atoms that form chemical bonds with other atoms become more stable or less stable?

    _____

SCIENCE CHALLENGE

When you look at a molecule of an everyday item such as sugar or salt, you are looking at a combination of elements. Using your library or the Internet, research common items you use every day, or ingredients of those items, to see if you can identify what elements they contain. In your Science Notebook, make a chart showing the name of the item, the molecule (ask your teacher for help if you cannot find the name of the molecule), and the elements within the molecule. Use the periodic table to help you identify the names of the elements in the molecule.

Vocabulary Review

PART A

Use these terms to fill in the blanks below.

chemical bond   electron   metallic bond   covalent bond

compound   element   neutron   isotopes

1. atomic particle that does not have a charge _____

2. same elements that have different numbers of neutrons _____

3. atomic particle with a negative charge _____

4. it cannot be reduced to simpler substances _____

5. material with two or more chemically combined elements _____

6. A _____ is a force that holds atoms together so they can combine and become more stable. Elements in gold, copper, and iron are held together by a _____ in which all of the electrons are shared by all of the atoms. A _____ holds together atoms that form molecules.

PART B

Complete each sentence using the correct term on the right. Some terms might not be used, and some may be used more than once.

atom

atomic mass

atomic number

elemental matter

ion

ionic bond

matter

product

7. The number of protons in an atom is its _____.

8. Three types of _____ are solids, liquids, and gases.

9. An _____ can have a positive or negative electric charge.

10. The _____ of an element is the total mass of its protons and neutrons.

SCIENCE EXTENSION

Draw a diagram in your Science Notebook showing the relationship between these terms: *chemical reaction, law of conservation of mass, reactant,* and *product.* Include definitions in your diagram.

Interpreting Diagrams

PART A

Draw a carbon atom as described below. Then label the following parts: nucleus, electron, proton, neutron.

Show 6 protons and 6 neutrons in the nucleus. Show two electrons in the inner energy level and four electrons in the outer energy level.

PART B

Use the periodic table shown above to answer the following questions.

1. Locate the element fluorine. What information about fluorine can you determine from the periodic table? _____

    _____

    _____

2. What can you say about how the mass of the elements changes from left to right and from top to bottom? Explain. _____

    _____

    _____

Reading Comprehension

PART A Matching

Lesson 3.3 describes changes in matter. There are two basic kinds of changes that can happen to matter: physical and chemical. Draw a line from each activity to the type of change it represents.

1. fold paper into a paper airplane   physical change

2. light a log in a fire pit

3. bake a cake

4. put a teaspoon of baking soda into a cup of vinegar   chemical change

5. sharpen a pencil in a pencil sharpener

PART B Arranging Atoms

Molecules that make up water can be arranged in a variety of different ways. In each of the following scenarios, the Adam family members are molecules of water that have gone through a change in state. Tell which state of matter the Adam family is in.

6. "We are so tightly packed that we cannot even move!" _____

7. "There is no way we can get ourselves into that jar; we are just too wide!" _____

8. "Hang on. We are spreading out all over . . . but at least we are not changing in volume!" _____

SCIENCE EXTENSION

Bonding Experience!
A television network introduces a new reality show called "Bonding Experience." The show profiles sets of real atoms and how they form bonds. Several sets of atoms arrived for the auditions. Help the producer figure out which bonding experience each set of atoms is demonstrating. Write *covalent*, *metallic*, or *ionic* under each diagram.

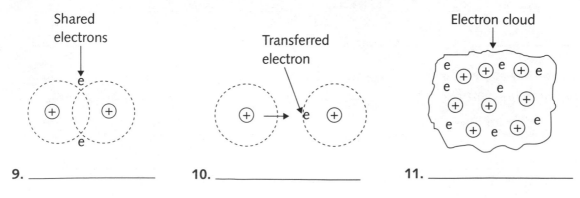

9. _____   10. _____   11. _____

Chemistry Connections: Acid Rain, Poisonous Precipitation

PART A

The chemical reaction below shows what happens when the sulfur released from burning coal reacts with water vapor in the atmosphere. The product is an acidic solution that falls to Earth as rain. Sometimes, the fallout can be airborne particles that settle as a deadly dust. Other times, an invisible cloud of acidic gas is the product.

$$SO_2 \text{ (gas)} \quad + \quad H_2O \text{ (liquid)} \quad \rightarrow \quad H_2SO_3 \text{ (in solution)}$$

sulfur dioxide   +   liquid water $\rightarrow$ sulfurous acid

Use the equation above to help you answer the questions below.

1. Are there the same number of atoms for each element on both sides of the chemical equation? _____

2. What are the reactants and products in this equation? Explain. _____

_____

3. How many molecules of product are shown in the equation? _____

PART B

Use what you have learned.

4. What is the smallest unit of an element that has all the properties of that element?

_____

5. To form a water molecule, H_2O, what does the oxygen atom share with each hydrogen atom?

_____

6. Is it possible to make a compound by combining a gas and a solid? _____

7. When mixed with water, acids and bases both break down. What does each release?

_____

SCIENCE EXTENSION

Get the Lead Out

Chemistry Connection The chemical symbol for lead is Pb, which comes from the Latin word for lead, *plumbum*. Looks like *plumbing*, right? In some very old houses, the water pipes contain lead. Lead is poisonous, so you do not want to drink water from lead pipes. You can buy charcoal (carbon) water filters to remove the lead. Some people believe that if you take an iron tablet, the iron will bond with the lead and flush it out of your body. Would you follow this advice? Develop a hypothesis. How would you test it?

Challenge Activity

Living things are made mostly from combinations of carbon, hydrogen, oxygen, and nitrogen. These elements, like all other elements, move from place to place on Earth. Any place that an element is stored is called a *reservoir*.

PART A   The Carbon Cycle

Carbon reservoirs

Carbon is stored in the atmosphere, bodies of water, soil, and living things. Carbon is also stored in fossil fuels (coal, oil, and natural gas) because these fuels are made from the remains of things that lived millions of years ago. Of these reservoirs, the ocean holds the most carbon, followed by fossil fuels. The atmosphere holds the least carbon.

Carbon movement between reservoirs

On land, carbon moves naturally between the atmosphere and living things. Animals breathe out a carbon-containing gas called carbon dioxide. Plants take this carbon dioxide out of the atmosphere and use it to make carbon-containing sugars. Humans and animals take in these sugars when they eat plants. When dead plants or animals decompose, carbon re-enters the atmosphere. Fossil fuels store carbon for a very long time—sometimes millions of years. When these fossil fuels are burned, carbon dioxide is released into the atmosphere.

Carbon also moves directly between the atmosphere and the ocean. Carbon dioxide actually helps to keep the pH of the ocean within a certain range. Carbon dioxide is also used by plants and by algae in the ocean. When these plants die, carbon may be released back to the atmosphere.

1. Think about your own home and the block or lot that you live on. List all of the things there that are parts of carbon reservoirs. _____

   _____

   _____

   _____

2. Look up information about carbon dioxide. Which type of chemical bond holds this molecule together? _____

   _____

   _____

   _____

3. Use the preceding information to draw a diagram in your Science Notebook of carbon flow between reservoirs. This flow is called the *carbon cycle*.

4. Do your own research to find and describe at least one other source from which carbon enters the atmosphere. _____

_____

_____

_____

_____

Carbon cycle terms

Scientists use particular terms when they talk about the carbon cycle. Use a dictionary or the Internet to help you figure out the meaning of these terms. Match the term on the left to its meaning on the right below.

5. reservoir   a.   a defined area that stores carbon

6. gigaton   b.   movement of carbon between reservoirs

7. flux   c.   time carbon spends in a reservoir

8. residence time   d.   an amount equal to 10^9 tons or 10^{12} kg of carbon

PART B   Physical and Chemical Changes

For each of the actions below, determine whether a physical change or a chemical change takes place. If you do not know the meaning of a word or term, use a dictionary to find out.

9. decay of animals or plants _____

10. release of liquid carbon dioxide from a fire extinguisher _____

11. burning of fossil fuels _____

12. burning of wood _____

13. dry ice turning into a gas _____

Key Concept Review

PART A Classify

Classify each substance below by writing it in the appropriate box.

steel	diamond	hematite	quartz
gold	sugar	pyrite	glass
coal	salt	concrete	water

Minerals

Not Minerals

PART B Comprehension

Answer each of the questions below on the lines provided.

1. How are minerals formed?

_____

2. Can solid substances made from plants be minerals? Explain.

_____

3. How is the chemical composition of a mineral written?

_____

4. What is specific gravity?

_____

5. What does the hardness of a mineral measure?

_____

SCIENCE CHALLENGE

There are many properties of minerals that are used to identify them, including color, luster, and density. Using your library or the Internet, research five minerals and list five properties of each mineral. Then make a matching game by providing a partner with a mixed-up list of the minerals you researched and a list of each mineral's properties. Your partner will give you his or her lists to match. See if you can match each mineral to its group of properties.

Vocabulary Review

PART A

Match the following definitions to one of the terms in the list below. Write the letter of the definition in the blank next to the term.

_____ 1. cleavage

_____ 2. density

_____ 3. fracture

_____ 4. hardness

_____ 5. inorganic

_____ 6. luster

_____ 7. magma

_____ 8. specific gravity

_____ 9. streak

a. melted rock beneath Earth's surface

b. the property in which a mineral breaks randomly

c. a description of how well a mineral reflects light

d. the ratio of a material's density to the density of water

e. substances that are not alive and are not made of plant or animal matter

f. a measure of how well a mineral resists being scratched

g. the property in which a mineral breaks smoothly and evenly along one or more planes

h. the color of a mineral when it is ground into a fine powder

i. how tightly the atoms are packed together in a mineral

PART B

Draw a diagram that shows the connections between these words: *mineral, crystal, ore,* and *gemstone.* Include definitions and examples of each word.

SCIENCE EXTENSION

Write two questions in the format: "What is _____?" using one of the vocabulary terms from the chapter for each blank. Exchange questions with your partner and answer the questions.

Graphic Organizer

PART A

Research one of the following minerals and then fill in the diagram: *amethyst, fluorite, sulfur, gold, halite, hematite,* or *zircon.*

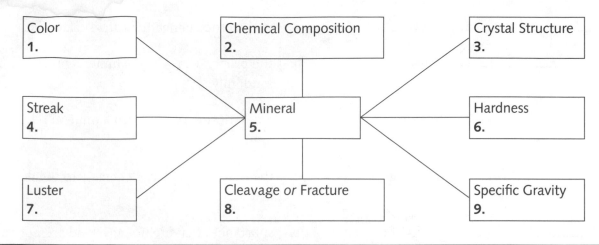

| Color 1. | Chemical Composition 2. | Crystal Structure 3. |

| Streak 4. | Mineral 5. | Hardness 6. |

| Luster 7. | Cleavage *or* Fracture 8. | Specific Gravity 9. |

PART B

Use the diagram above to help complete statements 10–13.

10. The chemical composition of _____ shows that it is _____

_____.

11. The hardness shows that _____ can scratch _____ and
    can be scratched by _____.

12. You know that _____ is a mineral because _____.

13. Minerals form when _____ cools and hardens, or when minerals
    that are dissolved in water are left behind during _____, or during
    the process of _____, when water cools or cannot hold any more
    dissolved substances.

SCIENCE EXTENSION

Write a short guide explaining which characteristics a person in the field might use to
identify a mineral, including what the person should look for.

Reading Comprehension

PART A

You have been asked to give a presentation on minerals to a classroom of students. To help you prepare, a list of possible questions that the students might ask is provided below.

1. Our house has lots of windows. It also has a basement made of concrete. My friend told me that glass and concrete are minerals. Are they? _____

   _____

2. I would like to find some minerals, but I do not live near any mines. I live near the ocean. Can I find any minerals near where I live? _____

   _____

3. My sister and I found some gold, but we are afraid it might be pyrite. How can we tell the difference between the two? _____

   _____

PART B

For the following pairs of words, explain the difference in their meanings as they relate to minerals.

4. cleavage and fracture _____

   _____

5. density and hardness _____

   _____

6. color and luster _____

   _____

SCIENCE EXTENSION

Body of Minerals

Did you know that minerals play an important role in keeping our bodies healthy?
Choose from the following mineral list to complete each sentence: iodine, fluoride, iron, calcium, sodium.

1. I drink milk because the _____ in milk helps build strong bones and teeth.

2. A lack of _____ can make a person anemic.

3. Most processed foods are high in _____, which increases the volume of fluid in a body.

Economic Connection: Mineral Resources

A nation's economy is influenced by its mineral resources. Diamonds make beautiful, precious jewelry and can also be used in industry. The fact that diamonds are so rare increases their value. But why are diamonds so rare? Well, you cannot find a diamond just anywhere. They develop under specific conditions and out of unpredictable events. At one point, South Africa was the world's leading producer of diamonds. How was it that this one spot on the planet came to have more diamond mines than any other country? Diamonds are formed in kimberlite pipes. A rare geologic event blasts magma from deep within Earth's interior toward the surface. The blast trail creates a kind of pipe. Most of the carbon that shoots up a kimberlite pipe turns into graphite. Every now and then, however, the carbon cools down under just the right conditions to become a diamond.

PART A

Choose a country other than the United States and prepare a short research report on its mineral resources. Use library resources and the Internet to find out which minerals the country has. How did those minerals form? How are they used? Are there any drawbacks to the uses of those resources? Summarize your findings and include a few statements about what effect mineral resources have on the economy of the country.

PART B

Use what you have learned to answer the following questions.

1. Recall the five characteristics that all minerals share. What can you assume about the structure of water molecules in frozen lake ice? _____

2. How do crystals form when magma hardens? _____

3. What holds more dissolved substances, hot water or cold water? _____

4. Where do minerals tend to break? _____

5. What kind of fracture makes smooth, curved surfaces? _____

SCIENCE EXTENSION

Kick the Can?

Economy Connection When a rock has a metallic element that is worth extracting, or taking out, then that rock is an ore. The metallic element aluminum is found in an ore known as bauxite. Soda cans are made from aluminum. The Jamaican economy relied on the money it earned from processing bauxite for aluminum. What do you suppose happened to Jamaica when the United States began recycling its aluminum cans? Find out where Jamaica is on a world map. How was the island nation formed? Is it possible that Jamaica has other valuable ores or mineral resources?

Chapter
4

Challenge Activity

PART A Jewelry Gemstones

Many minerals are made into jewelry. Some gemstones are listed below. For each one, do your own research to learn its properties. Then use this information to match each gemstone with the correct description.

Gemstone:

emerald	amethyst	topaz
ruby	sapphire	garnet

Description:

1. _____ This variety of quartz is purple. It has a white streak and a hardness of 7.

2. _____ This gemstone may be many colors but has a colorless streak. It is very hard. Its chemical formula is $Al_2SiO_4(F,OH)_2$.

3. _____ This is a variety of the mineral beryl and is green in color. It is harder than amethyst.

4. _____ This is a variety of corundum that is red. It is harder than topaz. Synthetic (human-made) forms of this material are also available.

5. _____ This variety of corundum might be pink or blue. Polished stones often have a starlike reflection in their center.

6. _____ This name actually refers to a group of similar minerals. One type, pyrope, is dark reddish-purple. Another type, alamandine, is more common. It is used in fine-grained sandpaper.

PART B Mineral Uses

People have been using minerals throughout human history. For example, minerals such as hematite were used to make paints well over 10,000 years ago. Not all minerals have had the same value to people, however. Which mineral do you think has been most important or has had the most influence on human culture? Do your own research and prepare an essay on your chosen mineral. What is it used for? Where is it found? Make sure to provide evidence of the mineral's impact on human life.

Rocks

Key Concept Review

PART A Outlining

As you read, fill in the outline below, using the main headings and subheadings of each lesson.

5.1: _____

   A. _____

   B. _____

5.2: _____

   A. _____

   B. _____

5.3: _____

   A. _____

   B. _____

   C. _____

5.4: _____

   A. _____

   B. _____

   C. _____

   D. _____

PART B Vocabulary

Circle the word that best completes each sentence.

1. (Sediment, Magma, Pumice) is made of rock particles transported by wind and water.

2. The sizes, shapes, and positions of the grains that make up a rock determine its (composition, texture, type).

3. Magma that pushes into surrounding rocks and cools underground forms (intrusive, extrusive, exclusive) igneous rock.

4. (Clastic, Chemical, Organic) sedimentary rocks form from the fragments of previously existing rocks.

SCIENCE EXTENSION

Different types of rock can be found in different areas of the world. The types of rock you will find as you walk along the beach will differ from the types of rock you might find near a volcano. Forces such as wind, water, and gravity, in addition to temperature, cause rocks to change and reform into new rocks. Choose an area of the world to research and write one or two paragraphs describing the types of rock that are typically found in this area. Be sure to describe how these rocks were formed.

Vocabulary Review

PART A

Use one of the terms from the word bank to complete each sentence below. Some words may be used more than once.

cementation	
composition	
deposition	
fossil	
rock	
rock cycle	
sediment	
texture	

1. A rock's _____ refers to the minerals that are found in it.

2. _____ is composed of rock particles and might also include bits of dead organisms and shells of sea animals.

3. During the ongoing process of the _____, rocks change from one type to another.

4. The size, shape, and position of the grains in a _____ describe its _____.

5. When _____ occurs, sediment falls to the ground or the bottom of a body of water. Then, through the process of _____, dissolved minerals in the water form crystals between the grains of

6. Sometimes a _____, the preserved remains of an organism, is found in a _____.

PART B

If a statement below is true, write *true* in the blank. If the statement is false, replace the underlined word with the letter of the phrase that makes it correct.

a. extrusive igneous rock　　**d.** chemical sedimentary rock　　**g.** contact metamorphism
b. intrusive igneous rock　　**e.** organic sedimentary rock　　**h.** hydrothermal metamorphism
c. clastic sedimentary rock　　**f.** regional metamorphism

_____ 7. Coal is a type of <u>chemical sedimentary rock</u> made from plants that lived millions of years ago.

_____ 8. <u>Contact metamorphism</u> occurs when water heated by volcanic activity changes the chemical composition of minerals and forms a new rock.

_____ 9. Magma that pushes into the surrounding rock and crystallizes underground forms <u>intrusive igneous rock</u>.

_____ 10. <u>Chemical sedimentary rock</u> is classified by the size of the particles of which it is composed.

SCIENCE EXTENSION

Design three signs that could be used in a rock shop to identify igneous, sedimentary, and metamorphic rocks.

Reading Comprehension

PART A

Decide which type of rock, *igneous, metamorphic,* or *sedimentary,* is being described. Then write the answer on the line provided.

1. one type is made of rock and mineral fragments called clasts _____

2. formed when high temperature and pressure change the texture, mineral makeup, or chemical makeup of a rock without melting it _____

3. the first stage in its formation is either chemical or physical weathering _____

4. can form when hot fluids come in contact with rocks _____

5. rocks that form when magma cools and crystallizes _____

6. a type formed when water evaporates and leaves behind dissolved minerals _____

7. can be identified by its mineral composition, ranging in color from light to dark _____

8. formed when tectonic plates collide, resulting in the folding of Earth's crust _____

9. intrusive types have a coarse-grained texture and extrusive types have a fine-grained texture _____

10. texture is foliated or nonfoliated _____

11. may have ripples, cracks, and pits from the effects of wind, water, and raindrops _____

PART B

In the blank next to the name of each rock, write *I* for igneous rock, *S* for sedimentary rock, and *M* for metamorphic rock.

_____ **12.** sandstone   _____ **14.** granite

_____ **13.** quartzite   _____ **15.** schist

SCIENCE EXTENSION

Write descriptions of two different rocks that could be classified as a type of igneous, sedimentary, or metamorphic rock. Trade descriptions with a partner and try to identify each rock.

Graphic Organizer

PART A Concept Map

In your Science Notebook, create a concept map using the following terms: *igneous, sedimentary, metamorphic, foliated, nonfoliated, organic, clastic, intrusive, extrusive, chemical, rocks.*

PART B Comprehension

Rocks on Earth's crust are constantly changing. Your textbook uses many new terms to describe how one rock type changes into another.

1. What is the relationship between *composition* and *texture?* Why are both texture and composition used by scientists to study the origin and history of rocks? _____

    _____

    _____

2. Explain the difference between *regional, contact,* and *hydrothermal* metamorphism.

    _____

    _____

    _____

3. If a clam dies in the sea, what type of rock does it help to form and how? _____

    _____

SCIENCE EXTENSION

One Lump or Two?

Dr. Ramirez plans to mine coal. Two methods used to mine coal today are surface mining and underground mining. Today, modern heavy equipment has reduced the physical demands that using pickaxes and shovels once required.

1. Why might it be important for Dr. Ramirez to know the geology of the coal deposit he plans to mine? _____

    _____

2. Dr. Ramirez chooses to use a form of surface mining. What makes this form of coal mining very noisy? _____

3. Dr. Ramirez knows there are a number of different ways surface mining causes environmental problems. List some of these problems. You may refer to the first case study at the end of this unit, *Mountains of Coal,* to help you. _____

    _____

Archaeology Connections: High-Tech Rocks

PART A

Archaeologists study the remains of ancient human cultures. They look for artifacts—items that people might have made out of natural resources. Artifacts made of metal or rock tend to survive over time. Ancient people valued obsidian for its ability to be cut, polished, and fashioned into tools, weapons, and ornaments. Obsidian is volcanic glass and can be cut into very sharp cutting edges. In fact, obsidian makes the best blades for surgical scalpels. It is hundreds of times sharper than surgical steel.

Complete the graphic organizer using these words: *large crystals, small crystals, high,* and *low.*

Granitic
light in color, contain quartz
and feldspar
1. _____ silica content
2. _____

Earth's Igneous Rocks

Basaltic
dark in color, contain magnesium
and iron
3. _____ silica content
4. _____

PART B

Use what you have learned.

5. If metamorphic rock melts again, what kind of rock does it become? _____

6. How is the rock cycle different from other cycles in nature? _____

7. The type of igneous rock that forms depends on two conditions. What are they?

_____

8. What happens to the resulting magma when temperatures are not high enough to melt all the minerals in a rock? Explain. _____

9. Do valuable minerals and gemstones form from intrusive or extrusive igneous rock? Explain. _____

10. For every kilometer beneath Earth's crust, the temperature rises by about 30°C. What is the temperature 200 kilometers underground? _____

SCIENCE EXTENSION

Archaeology Connection Archaeologists have found obsidian artifacts at sites many hundreds of miles from obsidian-rich outcrops. Such findings prove that ancient people must have traded, or had some sort of interchange with each other. Suppose you and a friend go rock hunting. The region contains mostly sedimentary rock, such as limestone. There are a few places when igneous rocks are exposed at the surface. You find a rock that is shiny and black. How could you determine what type of rock it is?

Challenge Activity

PART A **Famous Rocks**

There are many natural rock formations that are well-known because they are interesting to look at, significant events happened there, or some people consider them religious or spiritual places. There are also several famous rock carvings and human-made rock structures.

Some of these rocks are listed below. Do your own research to find information about each to fill in the table below. For one of the natural rock formations, find a picture and use it to draw and label a diagram.

Rock Formation/ Carving/Structure	Location	General Rock Type(s)	Rock Name(s)
Mt. Rushmore	South Dakota, U.S.A.	1. _____ and metamorphic	2. _____ and mica schists
Grand Canyon	3. _____	sedimentary	4. _____
Devil's Tower	5. _____ _____	6. igneous, surrounded by _____	phonolite porphyry
Uluru (formerly Ayer's Rock)	Uluru-Kata Tjuta National Park, central Australia	7. _____ _____	sandstone
Stonehenge	8. _____ _____	9. _____ and igneous	sandstone (sarsen stones), dolerite (bluestone)
Rock of Gibraltar	Gibraltar (south of Spain)	10. _____	11. _____
Mt. Kilimanjaro	12. _____	13. _____	basalts

PART B Earth's Crust Temperature

When sedimentary rock forms, deep layers of sediment experience higher temperatures than those closer to the surface. This is because the temperature of Earth increases with depth. This is called the *geothermal gradient*.

The amount that temperature changes with depth is slightly different from place to place on Earth. On average, for every kilometer below the surface (or 0.62 miles), the temperature beneath the crust rises by about 30°C. Use this information to solve the following problems.

14. If the temperature at the surface is 18°C, what is the temperature 1 km down?

_____

_____

_____

_____

15. If the temperature at the surface is 18°C, what is the temperature 5 km down?

_____

_____

_____

_____

16. If the temperature at the surface is 18°C, what is the temperature 10 km down?

_____

_____

_____

_____

Key Concept Review

PART A Sequencing

Number the following physical layers of Earth in the correct order, starting with the innermost layer. On the second blank, write a definition of the layer.

_____ _____ lithosphere

_____ _____ lower mantle

_____ _____ inner core

_____ _____ asthenosphere

_____ _____ outer core

PART B Comprehension

Read each of the questions about continental drift and answer them on the lines provided.

1. Explain the hypothesis of continental drift.

    _____

    _____

    _____

2. What theory provided the final piece of evidence for continental drift?

    _____

    _____

    _____

SCIENCE EXTENSION

The evidence supporting the theory of plate tectonics includes the shifting of Earth's tectonic plates as well as seafloor spreading. Using what you have learned about Earth's tectonic plates and their movement, make a prediction about the position of Earth's continents in one million years. Draw a map of Earth illustrating your hypothesis. Write a paragraph describing how conditions on Earth may change over one million years.

Vocabulary Review

PART A

Match each description in Column A with its term in Column B. Write the letter of the correct term in the space provided. Not all of the terms will be used.

Column A

1. _____ long, narrow valley formed when continental crust separates

2. _____ hanging wall of fault moves up relative to the footwall

3. _____ process by which an ocean plate is pushed down toward the lithosphere-asthenosphere boundary

4. _____ process by which one tectonic plate slips beneath another

5. _____ formed when large areas of land on one side of a fault drop down relative to the land on the other side

6. _____ process by which an ocean plate being pulled into the asthenosphere pulls the rest of the plate with it

Column B

a. convection
b. dome mountain
c. fault
d. fault-block mountain
e. folded mountain
f. normal fault
g. reverse fault
h. ridge push
i. rift valley
j. slab pull
k. slip-strike fault
l. subduction
m. volcanic mountain

PART B

Complete the cause-and-effect diagram using these words: *compression, deformation, shear stress, stress,* and *tension.* Define each word.

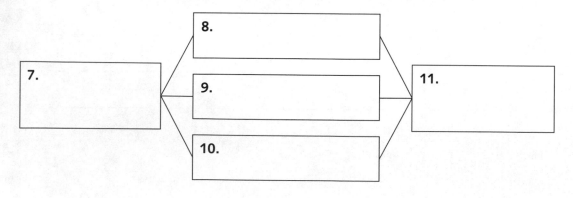

SCIENCE EXTENSION

Write a short dialogue in which three scientists define and relate the phrases *continental drift, seafloor spreading,* and the *theory of plate tectonics.*

Interpreting Diagrams

PART A

Label the diagram of Earth's layers using the following terms: *asthenosphere, core, crust, inner core, lithosphere, lower mantle, mantle,* and *outer core*.

Earth's Layers

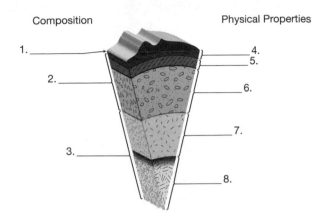

PART B

Match the words in the diagram to the descriptions below.

9. the very hot, solid part of the mantle _____

10. solid because of high pressure and mostly made of nickel _____

11. 5 km to 100 km thick with the continental part made of granitic rocks and the oceanic part made of basaltic rocks _____

12. layer of the upper mantle that slowly flows, like a piece of hot plastic _____

13. about 2,900 km thick and composed of rocks containing large amounts of iron and magnesium

_____

14. relatively cool, solid, brittle, and can crack and break _____

15. made up mostly of iron and nickel in liquid form _____

16. ball-shaped, with a diameter of about 7,000 km, made mostly of iron and nickel

_____

SCIENCE EXTENSION

Compare and contrast the three types of tectonic plate boundaries. Provide a geographic example of each.

Reading Comprehension

PART A **Chapter Summary**

Chapter 6 contains many details about Earth. Create a chapter summary in your Science Notebook. Label the subheadings with the lesson numbers and titles. Use bullet points under each lesson to record important information. Once you have completed the summary, compare yours with that of a classmate. If there are any differences, discuss why you chose the information that you did. Make revisions of your summary if needed.

PART B **The Big Breakup**

According to the hypothesis of continental drift, Pangaea, meaning "all Earth," was an ancient supercontinent that contained all of today's continents. Eventually, Pangaea broke into two pieces, Laurasia in the northern hemisphere and Gondwana in the southern hemisphere. Those pieces then split into seven main pieces. Complete the following diagram using the terms *Pangaea, Laurasia, Gondwana, Eurasia, Australia, Antarctica, North America, South America, Africa,* and *India.* Use a map to help you decide which piece each continent belonged to.

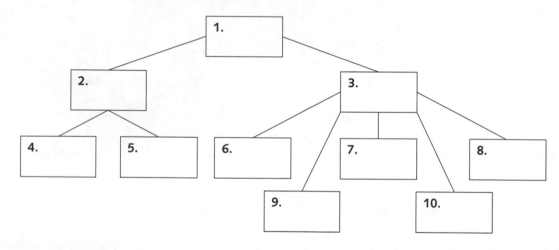

SCIENCE EXTENSION

Mountain Movements

Four mountains came together for a meeting. They are Mt. Fault-block, Mt. Dome, Mt. Folded, and the Volcanic Mountain. Decide which of the mountains made the following statements.

11. I was formed by new material being added to Earth's surface. _____

12. Even though getting where I am today was due to a lot of fractures, there is nothing I like better than blocks. _____

13. Once I reached my greatest height, these lovely peaks and valleys formed all over me.

Physics Connection: Heat Convection

PART A

When gaseous or liquid matter is heated, it expands and becomes less dense. This lighter heated matter rises while cooler, denser matter sinks. This movement of heated material is called convection. Label the drawing below to show which mantle currents are hot and which are cool.

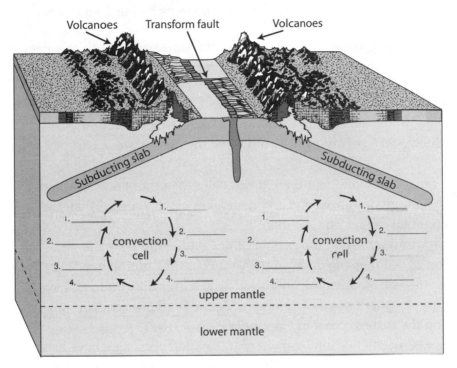

PART B

5. How does the convection created by different temperatures in the mantle cause tectonic plates to move?

_____

_____

6. Why is the material at the inner part of the mantle hotter than the material at the outer part of the mantle?

_____

_____

SCIENCE EXTENSION

Everyday Convection

Think of an example in which a heated liquid or gas causes convection currents. Describe this example in your Science Notebook.

Challenge Activity

PART A **Drifting Continents**

Imagine a fictional planet similar to Earth, with six continents and many oceans. Like Earth's continents, these continents were once part of a large land mass and have slowly moved apart over millions of years. Use the information below to determine the positions of the continents and label them A–F on the diagram. Use the same logic Wegener used to support his idea that Earth's continents had drifted apart.

For this exercise, assume that the continents have kept the same north-south orientation. In other words, the part of the land that was pointed north 225 million years ago is still pointed north today.

- Fossils of "plant a," which survives in warm, wet areas, have been found on Continent A, the western part of Continent D, and the northeastern part of Continent C.
- The mountain ranges on Continent E are much older than those on Continent D.
- The rocks in the mountain ranges on Continent F are much younger than the rocks in the mountain ranges on Continent E.
- Sedimentary rock formations on the east coast of Continent B have the same age and composition as sedimentary rock on the west coast of Continent F.
- 200 to 225-million-year-old fossils of "reptile a," which lives only on land, have been found on the northern coast of Continent A, the southern coast of Continent B, and the eastern coast of Continent E.
- Fossils of "reptile b," which lived in freshwater 150 million years ago, have been found on the northwestern coast of Continent A and the southeastern coast of Continent E.

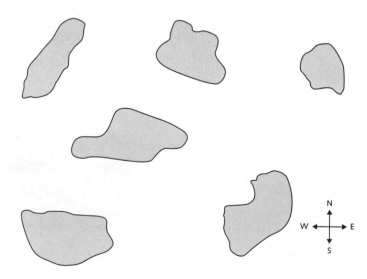

PART B Continental Mountains

Where are the tallest mountains in the world? The highest peaks on Earth's continents
are listed below. Do your own research to match the mountain with its altitude
(feet or meters above sea level). Then choose one mountain about which to do more
research. Write a well-developed paragraph about this mountain, explaining the
landscape and type of rocks around it; which mountain range, if any, it is part of;
and how this mountain range is thought to have been formed.

1. Denali/Mt. McKinley, North America   **a.** 20,320 feet, 6,194 meters

2. Mt. Kosciuszko, Australia   **b.** 22,834 feet, 6,960 meters

3. Mt. Everest, Asia   **c.** 7,310 feet, 2,228 meters

4. Mt. Kilimanjaro, Africa   **d.** 18,510 feet, 5,642 meters

5. Mt. Elbrus, Russia   **e.** 7,310 feet, 2,228 meters

6. Cerro Aconcagua, South America   **f.** 12,316 feet, 3,754 meters

7. Aoraki/Mt. Cook, New Zealand   **g.** 29,035 feet, 8,850 meters

Key Concept Review

PART A Vocabulary

Answer each question below using the correct term from the box. You will not use all of the terms.

epicenter	modified Mercalli scale	seismic gap
fault zone	moment magnitude scale	seismogram
intensity	Richter scale	seismometer
magnitude		

1. A section of an active fault that has not experienced significant earthquakes for a long period of time is called a _____.

2. The amount of energy released during an earthquake is measured by its _____.

3. The _____ rates the types of damage and other effects of an earthquake based on the observations of people who experienced it.

4. A _____ is a scientific instrument used to record seismic waves.

PART B Comprehension

Read each of the questions about earthquakes and answer them on the lines provided.

5. Where do earthquakes start?

_____

6. Which fault type results in the strongest earthquakes, and what kind of tectonic plate motion is characteristic of this type of earthquake?

_____

7. Name one difference between S-waves and P-waves.

_____

SCIENCE EXTENSION

In December 2004, a major earthquake in the Indian Ocean caused a tsunami that hit Asia and Africa. At least 225,000 people in eight countries perished in a few hours. The coastal areas of Indonesia and Sri Lanka and two Indian island chains bore most of the disaster. Using the Internet and other resources, as well as what you learned in this chapter, describe the earthquake and the effects on one of the areas listed above.

Vocabulary Review

PART A

Use one of the words or terms from the word box to fill in the blanks below.

earthquake	focus	seismic waves
elastic rebound	primary waves (P-wave)	surface waves
epicenter	secondary waves (S-wave)	tsunami
fault zones		

1. During _____, rocks suddenly return to their original shape, releasing the energy that causes a(n) _____.

2. The _____ of an earthquake is the place at which it occurs, and directly above it on the surface of Earth is the _____.

3. Most earthquakes occur near tectonic plate boundaries along areas called _____. If an earthquake causes vertical movement along the seafloor, it can generate a large, powerful wave called a(n) _____.

4. The energy released during earthquakes travels in _____, which feel like vibrations in the ground. _____ are felt first since they are the fastest, then _____, which move up and down or side-to-side, and finally _____, which move in two directions and cause the most damage.

PART B

Review the vocabulary terms in sections 7.2 and 7.3 and then complete the table.

Word or Phrase	Definition
intensity	5.
6.	a measurement that describes the amount of energy released during an earthquake
Richter Scale	7.
8.	uses factors to measure magnitude, such as the size of the fault at which the earthquake started, the stiffness of the rocks that broke at the fault, and the amount of movement along the fault

SCIENCE EXTENSION

Write a short story describing a day in the life of a seismologist and how and why the seismologist might use a seismometer and seismogram. Define *seismologist*, *seismometer*, and *seismogram* in your story.

Interpreting Diagrams

PART A

Label the diagram with these terms: *epicenter, fault, focus,* and *seismic waves.* Then answer the question that follows the diagram.

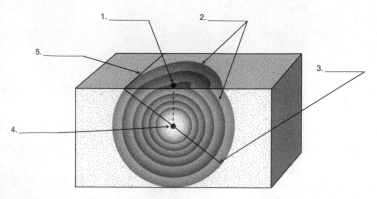

5. Where do earthquakes occur and what affects their location?

_____

_____

PART B

Identify whether each illustration is a P-wave, S-wave, or surface wave. Then complete the statements that follow the illustrations.

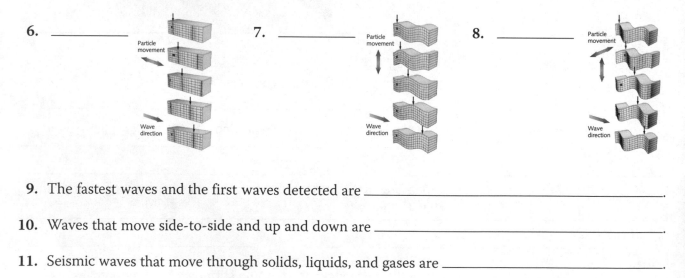

6. _____

7. _____

8. _____

9. The fastest waves and the first waves detected are _____.

10. Waves that move side-to-side and up and down are _____.

11. Seismic waves that move through solids, liquids, and gases are _____.

SCIENCE EXTENSION

Review Figures 7.12 and 7.14. Add a column to the modified Mercalli scale. Try to relate the moment magnitude scale to the modified Mercalli scale in the added column.

Reading Comprehension

PART A

You may have experienced earthquake-like shaking beneath you when walking over a bridge on which cars are driving. In your Science Notebook, create a K-W-L-S-H chart. In the column labeled *K*, write what you already know about earthquakes. In the column labeled *W*, write what you want to learn about earthquakes. After you have read the chapter, return to your chart and complete the remainder of the columns. Describe what you still want to learn about earthquakes in column *S*. Finally, describe ways that you can find this information in the *H* column.

PART B **Alike and Different**

Complete the following chart to help you distinguish similarities and differences between the three types of seismic waves: primary, secondary, and surface waves. Reread Lesson 7.1 if you need help.

	Primary Wave	Secondary Wave	Surface Wave
Nickname	1.	2.	3.
Speed	4.	5.	6.
Where they travel	7.	8.	9.
Describe movement	10.	11.	12.

SCIENCE EXTENSION

The ABCs of Earthquakes

Newspaper accounts, diaries, and letters from people who have experienced an earthquake can provide an understanding of the earthquake history of a region to help seismologists estimate future earthquakes. Today, you are a seismologist. People from the past have time-traveled to your home to give their accounts of an earthquake. Each person was told to describe the worst of what they saw or felt. For questions 13–16, use the modified Mercalli Intensity Scale on page 122 of your textbook to rate the earthquake that each person describes.

1. "My kids and I were indoors. We felt it, but my wife, who was outside, did not notice it. She did see our Model T car rock a bit." _____

2. "I was having trouble walking. My sister said that all of her pictures fell off the walls. Everyone we know felt the earthquake." _____

3. "I did not even know we had an earthquake. I read about it in the newspaper." _____

4. In your Science Notebook, explain how the descriptions in questions 13–15 could have been about the same earthquake.

Engineering Connection: Designing Earthquake-Resistant Buildings

PART A

After each feature, write how it would help buildings better resist earthquakes.

Earthquake Resistance Design Features:

1. reinforced concrete with interior steel rods or bars _____

   _____

2. cross-bracing with diagonal steel beams _____

3. base isolators made of steel and rubber built over the foundation _____

   _____

4. tall buildings anchored deeply in the ground _____

PART B

5. What kind of movement during an earthquake is most damaging to buildings?

   _____

6. Which type of structure has a better chance of surviving an earthquake, a very rigid or a very flexible structure? Explain.

   _____

7. What effect do you think large entrances or other openings on the first floor of a building would have on the strength of the building?

   _____

   _____

   _____

SCIENCE EXTENSION

Moving and Shaking

In this country, the states most likely to experience major earthquakes are Alaska, California, Hawaii, Nevada, and Washington. Why are these states most susceptible to earthquakes?

Chapter 7

Challenge Activity

PART A Measuring Magnitude

Scientists have used a variety of different scales for earthquake magnitude over the years, including the Richter scale, moment magnitude scale, and the modified Mercalli scale. The Richter scale is the original scale and was developed over 70 years ago. It is also called the *local magnitude scale.*

The Richter scale was designed to measure moderate-sized (magnitude 3 to 7) earthquakes in California. It best describes these earthquakes.

The moment magnitude scale was developed in 1978 by Dr. Thomas C. Hanks and Dr. Hiroo Kanamori. Moment magnitude can be determined using a seismogram. It can also be determined without a seismogram by taking other measurements at the fault where the earthquake occurred. The moment magnitude scale tends to be less variable than the Richter scale.

1. Which scale do you think would best describe a large-magnitude earthquake? Why?

_____

_____

_____

_____

2. When there are several different scale measures of an earthquake available, the United States Geological Survey reports moment magnitude. Why do you think they may prefer this scale?

_____

_____

_____

_____

_____

_____

_____

_____

In the next exercise, you might look at newspaper articles, magazines, or Internet reports about past earthquakes. Pay close attention to the magnitude of each earthquake. Which scale is the magnitude given in? If there is just a large M to describe the magnitude, or if the word *Richter* is not mentioned, it is probably moment magnitude. For example, a sentence starting "The 6.8-magnitude earthquake . . ." refers to moment magnitude, not the Richter scale.

PART B Past Earthquakes

Several devastating earthquakes are mentioned in Chapter 7 of your textbook. Choose one of these earthquakes or any past earthquake with a magnitude of more than 6. Use books or the Internet to learn more information about this earthquake. Where was the epicenter of this earthquake? What was its magnitude? Did it generate a tsunami? Prepare a poster presentation about this earthquake. Include pictures and descriptions of damage. Also include information about injuries or loss of life. Discuss what the area or city has done to recover and whether changes have been made to new buildings, roads, or freeways because of the earthquake.

_____

_____

_____

_____

_____

_____

_____

_____

_____

_____

_____

_____

_____

Key Concept Review

PART A   Classify

Classify each volcanic feature below by writing it in the appropriate box.

ash	gases	pillow lava
calderas	lava	pyroclastic materials
cinder cone volcanoes	lava plateaus	rock fragments
composite volcanoes	mid-ocean ridges	shield volcanoes
craters	pahoehoe lava	tephra

**Types of Volcanoes
and Formations**

Volcanic Materials

PART B   Comprehension

Read each of the questions below and answer them on the lines provided.
Use a separate piece of paper if necessary.

1. What kinds of gases are emitted by a volcano?

2. How can volcanoes, apart from the heat of lava, affect the environment around them?

3. How can volcanic ash be beneficial?

SCIENCE EXTENSION

How does a volcano affect weather? Is your area still experiencing the effects of any volcanic eruptions? How long does it take for the weather-related effects of a major volcanic eruption to disappear? Use the library, newspapers, and the Internet to research the most recent major volcanic eruption you can find. Write a paragraph describing its short-term and long-term effects on weather patterns.

Vocabulary Review

PART A

Decide whether each statement is true or false. If a statement is true, write *true* in the blank. If the statement is false, replace the underlined word or term with a word from the box that makes the statement true.

caldera	hot spot	shield volcano
cinder cone volcano	lava	tephra
composite volcano	magma	volcano
crater	pyroclastic material	

_____ 1.   Types of <u>pyroclastic material</u> include volcanic bombs and lapilli.

_____ 2.   <u>Lava</u> collects in a chamber below Earth's surface, and, as it becomes hotter and less dense, it rises to Earth's surface.

_____ 3.   A <u>crater</u> forms when an empty magma chamber collapses and creates a large depression in the ground.

_____ 4.   Basaltic lava forms the broad, gentle slopes of a <u>shield volcano</u>.

_____ 5.   A <u>volcano</u> is a vent on Earth's surface through which magma and other materials erupt.

_____ 6.   Volcanoes sometimes form at a <u>caldera</u>, which is a break in Earth's crust through which magma flows to the surface.

_____ 7.   <u>Tephra</u> flows onto Earth's surface or can be thrown upward in fountains. It can be thick or thin and includes types such as pahoehoe or aa.

PART B

Draw a diagram, such as a timescale, showing the relationship between active, dormant, and extinct volcanoes. Include definitions for each type of volcano.

SCIENCE EXTENSION

Write a short feature for a career guide describing the duties and working conditions of a volcanologist.

Interpreting Diagrams

PART A

Place the letter of the description below the correct diagram. Diagrams will have more than one letter below them.

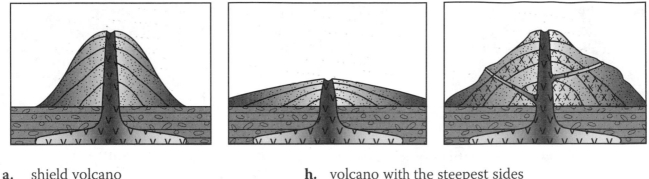

a. shield volcano

b. composite volcano

c. cinder cone volcano

d. has thick, granitic, slow-flowing lava

e. has basaltic lava that flows easily

f. the largest of the volcano types

g. this type often forms on the sides of other types of volcanoes

h. volcano with the steepest sides

i. forms from alternating layers of lava and volcanic rock and ash

j. has the least explosive eruptions

k. eruptions are violent

l. forms from ejected material that piles up around the vent

m. most often forms at hot spots

PART B

Complete the sentences.

1. Volcanoes that make up the Ring of Fire circle the _____ Ocean and are located at _____ boundaries where oceanic and _____ plates collide.

2. Explosive eruptions mostly produce _____, while nonexplosive eruptions mostly produce _____.

3. Factors that produce explosive eruptions include _____

_____.

SCIENCE EXTENSION

Describe the types of tephra you might find after an eruption, including the distance from the volcano of each type.

Reading Comprehension

PART A **K-W-L-S-H Chart**

Throughout history, people have found volcanoes both fascinating and frightening. Create a K-W-L-S-H chart in your Science Notebook. In column *K*, write what you already know about volcanoes. In the column labeled *W,* write what you want to learn. Return to your chart after reading the chapter. Complete the remainder of the columns by summarizing what you learned in the *L* column. Write what you still want to learn about volcanoes in column *S*. Then in the *H* column, write how you will find this information.

PART B

Lesson 8.1 introduces descriptions of volcanoes that might be new to you. It is helpful to keep these descriptions organized according to volcano. Organize the three major types of volcanoes—shield, cinder cone, and composite—in the chart below. Describe the shape, type of eruptions that occur, and the material that forms each type.

	Shield	Cinder cone	Composite
Shape	1.	2.	3.
Type of eruption	4.	5.	6.
Material that forms it	7.	8.	9.

SCIENCE EXTENSION
Good or Bad?

Volcanoes that erupt can cause a great deal of immediate damage as well as future damage. All this destruction may have a positive side to it. In each of the following scenarios, describe something bad and something good that could happen as a result.

1. A volcano erupts. Ash shoots into the air as high as 20 miles. Strong winds carry the ash around the world. _____

2. In Hawaii, the active volcano Kilauea, is a constant source of lava flowing into the ocean or into the direction of towns and villages. _____

Chapter 8

Biology Connection: Life After a Volcano

PART A

After a volcano erupts, life slowly re-establishes itself on the volcanic material left by the eruption. In the graphic organizer below, list three pioneer organisms that would initially return to the new volcanic rock.

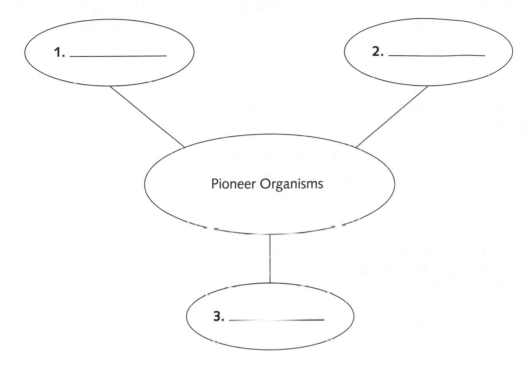

1. _____

2. _____

Pioneer Organisms

3. _____

PART B

4. How do these first plants or animals arrive?

_____

5. How do these pioneer species improve conditions so more organisms can live there?

_____

6. What types of organisms would likely come next in the successions of life on the volcanic material?

_____

SCIENCE EXTENSION

Back to Life

Areas of recent volcanic eruptions that receive a lot of precipitation and face the wind return to a forested state most quickly. Write a paragraph in your Science Notebook explaining why this is the case.

Challenge Activity

PART A Active Volcanoes

There are many active volcanoes on Earth. Pick one of these volcanoes and prepare a presentation about it. Draw a map of the area where the volcano is. Is this at a tectonic plate boundary, or is it a hot spot? In your presentation, explain what type of volcano this is and when it last erupted. If you can, find photos of the last eruption. Was there warning? How explosive was the eruption? Describe how many people live near this volcano and how their lives are affected by it. Remember that the volcano could have a positive effect, a negative effect, or both.

PART B Past Eruptions—Vesuvius

Mount Vesuvius has erupted several times in human history. Its most famous eruption was in August, A.D. 79. This eruption took people by surprise and destroyed the cities of Pompeii and Herculaneum (Ercolano).

The well-preserved ruins of these cities were discovered nearly 1,700 years later. Examining the ruins of these cities has allowed modern people to see what life was like in ancient times. Use books and the Internet to research Pompeii or Herculaneum. Where was this city? What types of things were found in the ruins?

Make a poster with information about the city. You may include information about Roman life at the time of the eruption, or a timeline of what scientists think happened during the eruption. Think about these things as you make your poster: Why didn't the people evacuate the cities? What were the main causes of death? How much ash or pyroclastic material covered the city? What types of structures are in the ruins, and how much damage did they have? Can people visit the ruins now?

Key Concept Review

PART A Sequencing

Number the following layers of soil or rock in the correct order, starting with the bottommost layer and moving upward. On the second blank, describe the layer in terms of how much humus it contains.

_____   _____ partly weathered bedrock

_____   _____ topsoil

_____   _____ subsoil

PART B Comprehension

Read each of the questions about weathering and answer them on the lines provided.

1. What is mechanical weathering?

_____

_____

_____

2. What causes mechanical weathering?

_____

_____

_____

3. How does abrasion weather rocks?

_____

_____

_____

_____

SCIENCE EXTENSION

Soil is a valuable resource, and, like many resources, its misuse or overuse can result in its loss. Research and describe how the combination of weathering and human intervention has caused the loss of soil. Describe how this loss has affected communities and explain what can be done to minimize the loss of this valuable resource.

Chapter 9

Weathering and Soil Formation

Vocabulary Review

PART A

Match each term in Column B with its description in Column A. Write the letter of the correct term in the space provided.

Column A

1. _____ Water fills a crack in a rock, freezes, and widens the crack.

2. _____ the layers of rock beneath soil

3. _____ the chemical reaction between oxygen and other substances

4. _____ the transport of substances downward through soil

5. _____ rain that contains acid because of air pollution

Column B

a. acid precipitation

b. bedrock

c. frost wedging

d. leaching

e. oxidation

PART B

Draw a diagram relating these terms: *weathering, chemical weathering, differential weathering,* and *mechanical weathering.* Define each word and give an example.

SCIENCE EXTENSION

Write a short paragraph using two to four new vocabulary words from the chapter to describe weathering or soil formation. Leave blanks where these new words would be. Exchange paragraphs with a partner and fill in the blanks.

Interpreting Diagrams

PART A

Identify and label the layers of the soil profile using the words or phrases below.

Horizon A	determines the type of soil that forms
Horizon B	composed of partially weathered bedrock or transported soil
Horizon C	contains leached nutrients and minerals
Bedrock	partly weathered parent material
subsoil	has the most humus
topsoil	

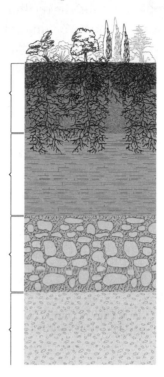

PART B

Describe the mechanical or chemical weathering that could occur in each of the situations below.

1. Rocks fall in a *falling rock area* along the sides of a highway. _____

    _____

2. Moss grows on stepping stones in a lawn. _____

    _____

3. Oxygen combines with iron in rocks. _____

    _____

4. Water repeatedly freezes and melts in the crack of a rock. _____

    _____

SCIENCE EXTENSION

Describe the factors in your region that would affect the rate of weathering on a birdbath made of granite.

Reading Comprehension

PART A Identifying Relationships

Look at the terms and phrases below. Match two that seem to go best together. Then, in your Science Notebook, describe the relationship between the two terms or phrases. Do this for all the terms in the box. You might benefit from rereading Lesson 9.1.

abrasion	carbonic acid	dissolve	grinding	oxygen	rust
absorb minerals	caves	exfoliation	lichens	pressure	water

PART B Cause and Effect in Soil Conservation

Soil is a loose mixture of rock and mineral fragments, organic material, water, and air. One way to protect soil is by using good gardening practices. In your Science Notebook, create a cause-and-effect chart for each form of soil conservation listed below. Include the factors listed next to each. Refer to Lesson 9.3 if you need help.

Crop rotation: same crop, deplete, different crop, nutrients
Contour plowing: erosion, rainwater, slope, curves
Cover crops: main crop, deplete, harvest, nutrients, decay

SCIENCE EXTENSION

Shake It Up!

Harold collected 30 rough, jagged stones that were all about the same size, three containers with lids labeled *A*, *B*, and *C*, and three clear jars. He put 10 stones into each container and then added enough water to each to fill each halfway. He shook container A 10 times and then poured the water into one of the clear jars. Harold then shook container B 100 times and then poured the water into another clear jar. Harold did not shake container C, but did pour the water into the third clear jar. How do you think the water in each of the clear jars differed? What type of weathering does Harold's experiment demonstrate?

_____

_____

_____

_____

_____

Biology Connection: Decomposers and Soil Formation

PART A

List four organisms that are decomposers.

1. _____   2. _____

Decomposers

3. _____   4. _____

PART B

5. Why are decomposers so important in the web of life?

_____

6. Which part of soil has the largest amount of decomposed plant and animal matter?

_____

7. Soils from which type of climate contain the most organic matter?

_____

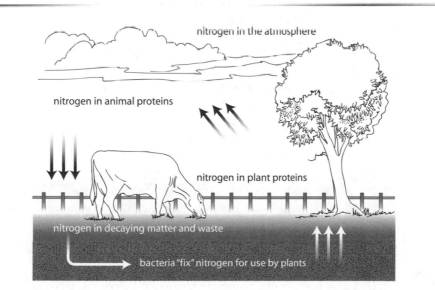

nitrogen in the atmosphere

nitrogen in animal proteins

nitrogen in plant proteins

nitrogen in decaying matter and waste

bacteria "fix" nitrogen for use by plants

SCIENCE EXTENSION

The Nitrogen Cycle

This illustration shows how the nitrogen cycle works. In your Science Notebook, explain how decomposers and nitrogen-fixing bacteria work together in the nitrogen cycle.

Challenge Activity

PART A   The Nitrogen Cycle

Nitrogen is a valuable nutrient for living things. Plants get the nitrogen they need in order to grow from the soil; animals get the nitrogen they need by eating these plants.

Like carbon, nitrogen cycles through the environment. Research the nitrogen cycle and use the information you find to fill in the simplified diagram of the nitrogen cycle below. For each blank space, fill in the letter that describes what is happening.

a.   Animal waste and decay put nitrogen into the soil.

b.   Nitrogen in the atmosphere reacts with oxygen in the presence of lightning. This forms the compounds nitric oxide (NO) and nitrogen dioxide (NO_2).

c.   Certain specialized bacteria live symbiotically with plants called *legumes* (legumes include beans, peas, alfalfa, and clover). These bacteria take nitrogen from the air and change it into nitrogen-containing compounds that plants can use.

d.   NO and NO_2 react with rainwater to form nitric acid (HNO_3), which falls to the ground with rain. This is one way nitrogen gets into soil.

e.   Animals get nitrogen from eating plants.

f.   Bacteria in the soil change nitrogen from animal waste into a form plants can use.

g.   Some special soil bacteria change nitrogen-containing compounds in the soil into nitrogen gas, which is released into the air.

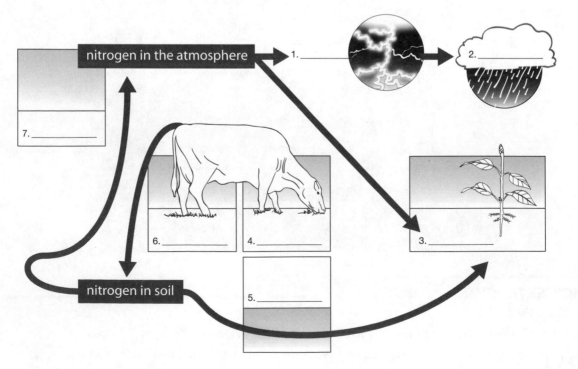

PART B Weathering and Rock Formations

The United States has many unique rock formations that have been shaped by weathering. Interesting examples are the rock arches in Arches National Park, Utah. Do your own research on these arches or a different rock formation made by weathering. What type or types of rock is it? Which weathering processes have affected the rock? What is the surrounding soil like? Write your findings in a well-developed paragraph. Find pictures and use these pictures to make a diagram of the rock formation. Label areas where evidence of physical or mechanical weathering is visible.

Name _____ Date _____ Class _____

Key Concept Review

PART A Outlining

As you read, fill in the outline of the chapter below using the main headings and subheadings of each lesson.

10.1: _____

   A. _____

   B. _____

   C. _____

   D. _____

   E. _____

   F. _____

   G. _____

   H. _____

   I. _____

10.2: _____

   A. _____

   B. _____

   C. _____

   D. _____

   E. _____

   F. _____

   G. _____

10.3: _____

   A. _____

   B. _____

   C. _____

   D. _____

10.4: _____

   A. _____

   B. _____

   C. _____

PART B Vocabulary

Circle the word that best completes each sentence below.

1. Large masses of ice are called (loess, glaciers, deltas).

2. A narrow bank of sand that forms as a spit grows and extends across a body of water is called a (longshore bar, baymouth bar, spit).

3. A steep, pyramid-shaped peak formed when glaciers have eroded three or more sides of a mountaintop is called a(n) (cirque, arete, horn).

SCIENCE EXTENSION

Erosion can be caused by water, glaciers, wind, and gravity. Choose one type of erosion. Research its effect on a particular area of the world. Describe the landscape features affected by erosion and how the erosion has affected surrounding communities or habitats.

Vocabulary Review

Fill in the blanks of the puzzle using words from the following list:

arete	delta	gully	loess	slump
cirque	dune	horn	moraine	spit
creep	eskers	lahar	outwash	till

1. narrow bank of sand that projects into the water __ __ __ __

2. sediment carried and deposited by meltwater streams __ __ __ __ __ __ __

3. narrow, bladelike ridge __ __ __ __ __

4. triangular-shaped deposit of silt and clay __ __ __ __ __

5. deposit of fine, wind-blown silt __ __ __ __ __

6. a cup-shaped depression formed by a landslide __ __ __ __ __

7. unsorted material deposited by glaciers __ __ __ __

8. bowl-shaped depression on the side of a mountain __ __ __ __ __ __

9. fast mudflow caused by volcanic eruption __ __ __ __ __

Match the following definitions to one of the terms in the list. Write the letter of the definition in the blank next to the term.

a. glaciers that form in high, mountainous areas

b. skipping or bouncing motion of particles

c. long ridges of sand separated from the mainland and shaped by longshore currents

d. sandbar in front of most beaches

e. the place where land and a body of water meet

f. method of transportation by which particles are carried long distances in air

10. _____ barrier island

11. _____ shoreline

12. _____ longshore bar

13. _____ suspension

14. _____ saltation

15. _____ valley glacier

SCIENCE EXTENSION

Write three clues each that could be used to identify two new vocabulary words in this chapter. Exchange clues with a partner and identify the words.

Interpreting Diagrams

PART A

Identify and label the following landforms on the appropriate diagram: barrier island, baymouth bar, lagoon, sea arch, sea stack, spit, tombolo, wave-cut cliff, and wave-cut terrace.

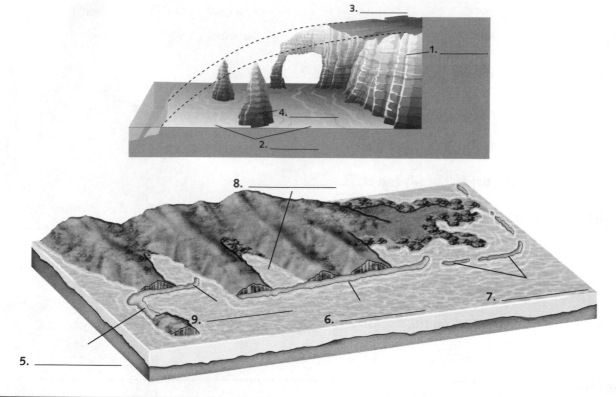

PART B

Complete the chart on erosion and deposition.

Source	Erosion Characteristics	Erosion Landform Features	Deposition Landform Features
Running water	10.	11.	12.
Waves	13.	14.	15.
Glaciers (Valley and Continental)	16.	17.	18.
Wind	19.	20.	21.
Gravity	22.	23.	24.

SCIENCE EXTENSION

Draw and label a diagram that shows one of the landform features in the chart above.

Write a short description of the process that resulted in the landform.

Reading Comprehension

PART A **Matching**

Match each erosion or deposition feature with the correct process that formed it.
Write the letter on the line next to the correct word. Each letter may be used more
than once.

1. glacier erosion _____

2. glacier deposition _____

3. water erosion _____

4. water deposition _____

5. mass movement _____

6. wind erosion _____

7. wind deposition _____

a. gulley

b. drumlin

c. delta

d. ventifact

e. desert pavement

f. striations

g. sand dune

h. alluvial fan

i. moraine

j. U-shaped valley

k. slump

l. V-shaped valley

m. loess hills

n. mudflow

PART B **The Human Impact**

The impact of erosion and deposition can be seen throughout the world. People can
increase or decrease the speed of natural erosion processes. Read the statements
below and explain how erosion will be affected. If you need to, refer back to the
chapter for help.

8. A tropical forest is cut down, exposing the soil. _____

_____

9. A breakwater is built parallel to a beach. _____

_____

10. A road is built through a mountain pass, exposing rock walls above the road. _____

_____

SCIENCE EXTENSION

What Is Creep?

Of all the types of mass movement, creep is the most difficult to observe in action.
Imagine a tree that has been affected by creep. Draw pictures of what the tree, its roots,
and the soil might look like before and after it was affected by creep.

Art Connection: Art Inspired by Landforms

PART A

The drawing below shows Cathedral Peak in Yosemite National Park.

1. What type of landscape feature is Cathedral Peak?

    _____

2. What kind of erosion created it?

    _____

PART B

Many artists have painted and photographed the beautiful mountain ranges and glacial landforms in Yosemite and elsewhere. Ansel Adams is the artist most associated with Yosemite National Park. He is well known for his beautiful black-and-white landscape photographs. Use the library or the Internet to find landscape photographs of Yosemite National Park taken by Ansel Adams. Choose one photograph that you like and answer the following questions:

3. What is the name of the photograph, and what is it a photograph of?

    _____

4. What type of landform is shown in the photograph, and how do you think it was formed?

    _____

SCIENCE EXTENSION

Down in the Valley

Imagine that you are hiking in the mountains, and you come across a wide, U-shaped valley. Explain, in your Science Notebook, how this valley most likely was formed.

Challenge Activity

Crossword Puzzle

The purpose of this exercise is to become familiar with terms used to describe erosion and deposition. The crossword puzzle below contains terms about erosion and deposition. Use the clues to fill in the crossword. Where there is a word in the puzzle but no clue, write a clue.

Grid (across words): 1 LAGOON, 3 TOMBOLO; 6/7 KETTLEHOLE; 11 DRUMLIN (down starting at 11D: D R U M L I N); numbered cells 2A, 4B, 5, 8, 9, 10, 12, 13, 14, 15L, 16.

Across:

1. _____

3. _____

5. This water flowing alongside a shoreline can create dangerous conditions for swimmers.

6. _____

9. a ridge made out of till

10. The Twelve Apostles in Western Victoria, Australia, are examples of this type of landform that has been carved by waves.

13. In Glacier National Park, Montana, the Garden Wall is an example of this type of landscape feature carved by a glacier.

14. In the United States, these shifting sand hills can be seen along the shores of the Great Lakes.

15. The plants that grow in this type of soil are likely to be large and healthy.

16. This kind of mass movement brought down the Old Man of the Mountain rock formation in New Hampshire in 2003.

Down:

2. This type of mass movement might occur in the Swiss Alps, the Himalayas, and the Rocky Mountains.

4. These landforms protect wetlands and marshes, and they provide a place for many plants and animals to live.

7. This sudden movement can trigger landslides.

8. Striations on rock surfaces are caused by movement of these ice masses.

10. Material that is carried by water or settles to the bottom of a body of water

11. _____

12. This pavement can be found in Joshua Tree National Park in southern California.

Key Concept Review

PART A **Classify**

Label the graphic organizer below with two titles: "Relative Dating" and "Absolute Dating." Then classify each term below by writing it in the appropriate box.

tree rings	carbon-14	original horizontality
inclusion	correlation	radiometric dating
radiocarbon dating	half-life	
superposition	cross-cutting relationships	

_____   _____

PART B **Comprehension**

Read each of the questions below and answer them on the lines provided.
Use a separate piece of paper if necessary.

1. What is a fossil? _____

_____

2. Define trace fossil and give an example of a trace fossil. _____

_____

3. What does the principle of cross-cutting relationships state? _____

_____

4. How are index fossils used? _____

_____

5. The half-life of carbon-14 is 5,730 years. How many years does it take
   for an organism to lose half of its original supply of carbon-14? _____

SCIENCE EXTENSION

There are many different types of fossils. Use the library or Internet to identify
at least three types of fossils and write a paragraph describing each one. Include
the following information: the type of organism, how the fossil was formed,
where it was found, and how old the fossil is.

Vocabulary Review

PART A

Use terms from the list below to fill in the blanks.

absolute dating	half-life	radioisotope
dendrochronology	radiocarbon dating	radiometric dating

1. _____ is any method used to determine the actual age of a layer of rock or fossil by using a _____, which decays through radiation.

2. The _____ of a radioactive sample is the time that it takes for one-half of the sample to decay.

3. _____ uses carbon-14 to determine the age of a fossil.

4. Other _____ methods include _____, which is the comparison of yearly growth rings in trees.

PART B

Decide whether each statement is true or false. If a statement is true, write *true* in the blank. If the statement is false, replace the underlined word with the letter of the word or phrase that makes it true.

a. carbonaceous film	**d.** inclusion	**g.** permineralization
b. cast	**e.** index fossils	**h.** petrification
c. correlation	**f.** mold	

_____ 5. <u>Relative dating</u> is a method used to match rock layers from different geographical areas.

_____ 6. <u>Cross-cutting relationships</u> use intrusions, which are bands of rocks that cut across sedimentary rock layers and are younger than the rock layers they cut across.

_____ 7. A <u>mold</u> is a type of fossil in which sediments fill the hollow space in rock that has the shape of the organism or its parts, and then hardens into rock.

_____ 8. One way to date rock layers relatively is to use <u>trace fossils</u>.

SCIENCE EXTENSION

Write a set of five questions that could be used to interview a paleontologist. Use at least four new vocabulary words to write the questions. Then write the answers you think the paleontologist would give.

Interpreting Diagrams

PART A

Use relative dating principles to number the rock layers and the igneous intrusion in order from oldest to youngest on the lines provided (1=oldest; 10=youngest). On your own paper, write a short paragraph describing the history of deposition in this area.

PART B

1. Name two layers in the diagram above that can be used to illustrate the principle of superposition. Explain. _____

_____

2. Name at least two layers that can be used to illustrate the principle of cross-cutting relationships. Explain. _____

_____

3. Between which layers does an unconformity occur? Explain. _____

_____

SCIENCE EXTENSION

Write a short field guide that explains what to look for when hunting for fossils in the field. Use drawings to illustrate the types of fossils.

Reading Comprehension

PART A

Compare and Contrast Using what you have learned in Chapter 11, compare and contrast the following terms.

1. *mold* and *cast:* _____

   _____

   _____

   _____

2. *permineralization* and *pertrification:* _____

   _____

   _____

   _____

3. *relative dating* and *absolute dating:* _____

   _____

   _____

   _____

PART B

Ariana, a paleontologist at Science University, has several fossils and other remains in her lab. Name the method Ariana should use to determine the age of each of the artifacts listed below.

4. a thick piece of rock from the bottom of a lake _____

5. a photo of an outcrop showing several rock layers _____

6. a fossil of a snail _____

7. a fossil of a dinosaur _____

SCIENCE EXTENSION

Walter, a scientist, has found a large number of fossils in one area. By using radiocarbon dating, he has discovered that most of the organisms died around the same time. What methods could he use to find out more about what caused these organisms to die? On your own paper, write a paragraph explaining how he would use them.

Environment Connection: Fossil Fuels

PART A

Fossil fuels include oil and natural gases that formed over millions of years from the remains of prehistoric organisms. When fossil fuels are burned, they release energy that can be used to produce electricity, heat, and power for vehicles. They are also used to make plastics and other materials.

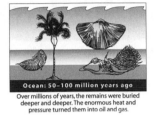

Ocean: 50–100 million years ago

Over millions of years, the remains were buried deeper and deeper. The enormous heat and pressure turned them into oil and gas.

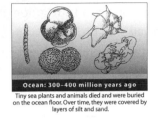

Ocean: 300–400 million years ago

Tiny sea plants and animals died and were buried on the ocean floor. Over time, they were covered by layers of silt and sand.

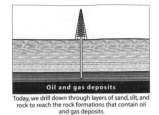

Oil and gas deposits

Today, we drill down through layers of sand, silt, and rock to reach the rock formations that contain oil and gas deposits.

Use the information shown above to answer the following questions:

1. How many years did it take for oil and gas to form? _____

2. Why do you think oil and gas are called fossil fuels?

_____

PART B

All countries depend on fossil fuels. The graph below shows how many gallons of crude oil from a 44.6 gallon barrel are used to make the products listed.

Use the graph to answer the following questions:

3. What percentage of crude oil is used to produce gasoline?

_____

4. Based on this graph, what would be the most effective thing a person could do to reduce the amount of oil he or she consumes?

_____

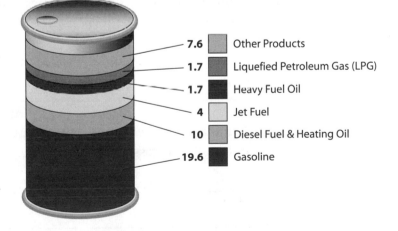

- **7.6** Other Products
- **1.7** Liquefied Petroleum Gas (LPG)
- **1.7** Heavy Fuel Oil
- **4** Jet Fuel
- **10** Diesel Fuel & Heating Oil
- **19.6** Gasoline

SCIENCE EXTENSION

Based on what you have learned about oil and gas reserves, write a paragraph explaining why you think they are nonrenewable energy sources.

Challenge Activity

PART A Fossils in Public Lands

Many fossils have been found in places that are state and national parks. For example, Petrified Forest National Park in Arizona is named for the wide variety of petrified wood it contains. New fossils are continually discovered there.

Do your own research about state and national parks. Choose a park in which fossils can be seen or have been found. Imagine that you are a tour guide and want to bring a group of visitors to the area. Write an informational brochure about what they might see. Include the types of fossils, a brief description of how they were formed, and what information the fossils give about the park's natural history. Also include a set of rules for visiting the park. Should visitors take fossils from the park? Why or why not?

PART B Absolute Dating

Radiocarbon Dating

Plants and animals constantly take in carbon, some of which is carbon-14. In a living organism, the ratio of carbon-14 to carbon-12 is about the same as it is in the air. Once an organism dies, the amount of carbon-14 in its body decreases as time passes.

1. If the ratio of carbon-14:carbon-12 in the air when a small animal is alive is $1:10^{12}$, or 1:1 trillion (also written as 1×10^{12}), what is the ratio of carbon-14 to carbon-12 in the animal's body? _____

    _____

    _____

2. Imagine that this animal dies, and its body becomes a fossil. In 5,730 years, what will be the ratio of carbon-14 to carbon-12?

    _____

    _____

3. If this fossil was found at a time when the ratio of carbon-14 to carbon-12 was 1:8 trillion, how old would the fossil be? _____

    _____

    _____

Radiometric Dating

Several radioisotopes are used in radiometric dating. The table below shows some of these radioisotopes. For each of the radioisotopes, find their half-lives, and put this information into the table.

Radioisotope	Half-life
Carbon-14	5,730 years
Rubidium-87	**4.**
Potassium-40	1.26 billion years
Samarium-147	**5.**
Thorium-232	**6.**
Uranium-235	**7.**
Uranium-238	**8.**

9. Considering the information you found, why do you think getting rid of radioactive waste is such a delicate and complicated process?

_____

_____

_____

_____

_____

_____

_____

_____

_____

_____

_____

Chapter 12

Geologic Time

Key Concept Review

PART A Sequencing

Number the following geologic time periods in the correct order, starting with the oldest at the bottom and continuing to the most recent. On the second blank, name one characteristic or event from that time period.

_____ _____ Cenozoic Era

_____ _____ Precambrian Time

_____ _____ Mesozoic Era

_____ _____ Paleozoic Era

PART B Comprehension

Read each of the questions about geologic time and answer them on the lines provided.

1. What major event do the Mesozoic and Paleozoic Eras have in common?

   _____

2. Which type of animal benefited from Earth becoming hotter and drier during the Paleozoic Era, and how did they adapt?

   _____

   _____

3. During which period did Earth experience its last ice age?

   _____

4. Which period marks the development of the largest dinosaurs?

   _____

5. Human beings are members of which species?

   _____

SCIENCE EXTENSION

The evolution of living things through time shows how they can adapt to different environments. Changes in habitat, temperature, and availability of food sources all have an effect on how living things evolve. Choose one subgroup of animals from either the vertebrate or invertebrate group and trace its development through geologic time. How did it adapt to changes in its environment? Use the library and the Internet to help you with your research.

Vocabulary Review

PART A

Match each term in Column B with its description in Column A. Write the letter of the correct term in the space provided.

Column A	Column B
1. _____ the condition of a species when all of its members die	**a.** adaptation
2. _____ The environment has an effect on the ways species evolve.	**b.** bipedal
3. _____ an animal with a backbone	**c.** cyanobacteria
4. _____ a trait that helps a species survive and reproduce	**d.** evolution
5. _____ an order of mammals including humans, apes, and monkeys	**e.** extinct
6. _____ a change in characteristics passed on from one generation to another as a result of environmental change	**f.** hominid
7. _____ humans and human ancestors	**g.** natural selection
8. _____ walks upright on two legs	**h.** primate
9. _____ single-celled, ocean-dwelling organisms	**i.** vertebrate

PART B

Complete the diagram relating these terms: *eon, epoch, geologic time scale, era,* and *period.* Define each word and give an example of each.

> **10.** _____

Each time unit in the scale is
divided into a smaller unit of time.

> **11.** _____ → **12.** _____ → **13.** _____ → **14.** _____

SCIENCE EXTENSION

Describe three events that took place during one of the following periods: Triassic Period, Jurassic Period, Cretaceous Period, Paleogene Period, or Quaternary Period. Exchange descriptions with a partner and identify the period that your partner has described.

Graphic Organizer

PART A

Provide the years and missing names for eons, eras, or periods in the chart below.

Years Ago	Eon	Era	Period	Events
2.	**5.**	**8.**	**12.**	**21.**
			Neogene	
			11.	**20.**
		7.	Cretaceous	**19.**
			10.	**18.**
			9.	**17.**
		6.	Permian	
			Pennsylvanian	
			Mississippian	
			Devonian	**16.**
			Silurian	
			Ordovician	**15.**
			Cambrian	**14.**
1.	**4.**	Precambrian Time		**13.**
3.8 billion	**3.**			
4.6 billion	Hadean			

PART B

Write the letter of an event description in the correct numbered space above.

a. Dinosaurs become the dominant animals, but insects evolve too.

b. Ice age ends, and *homo sapiens* evolve.

c. Angiosperms, or flowering plants, evolve, and so do ants, termites, and bees.

d. Pangaea starts to break apart and conifers, Earth's largest plants, evolve.

e. Single-celled, ocean-dwelling organisms called cyanobacteria emerge.

f. Fishes, including armor-plated fishes and large, jawless fishes, become common.

g. Trilobites dominate the oceans.

h. Organisms similar to lichens evolve on land, and then land plants follow.

SCIENCE EXTENSION

Draw a diagram to compare and contrast events that occurred during two geologic time periods from the same era.

Reading Comprehension

PART A **That Happened *Why?***

At this time, Earth is the only known planet to be inhabited by life-forms. Conditions had to be just right for living things to develop. The following statements describe the factors that contributed to the development of life on Earth. Match each statement with the phrases that support them by writing the correct letters on the lines provided. Refer to Lesson 2.1 in your book.

1. changing landscapes and position of oceans and shorelines _____

2. life-forms evolve as a result of a specific event _____

3. creates a magnetic field, which shields the planet from dangerous ultraviolet rays _____

4. Water is present in a liquid state. _____

a. iron core

b. Earth's position in the solar system

c. movement of tectonic plates

d. specific time in Earth's history

PART B **That Happened *When?***

Chapter 12 discusses the different ways we define geologic time and when important developments occurred. Identify when each event occurred starting with the period, then the era, and finally the eon.

5. mass extinction of the last of the dinosaurs _____

6. The number of land vertebrates increases greatly for the first time. _____

7. The first land plants evolve. _____

8. mass extinction, which may have been caused by worldwide cooling _____

9. The first fossil human bones are discovered. _____

10. Dinosaurs become Earth's dominant animals. _____

11. Conifers become Earth's largest plants. _____

12. the Cambrian Explosion _____

Biology Connection: Plant Evolution

PART A

Number these plants or plantlike organisms in the order in which they evolved and appeared on Earth.

_____ ferns

_____ seaweed

_____ flowering plants

_____ conifers

_____ cyanobacteria

_____ lichens

PART B

1. Choose one of the plants from Part A and explain why it might have evolved from the other plants. What is a structure or characteristic that helped it survive and spread?

    _____

    _____

    _____

2. Why do you think that bees and flowering plants evolved at the same time?

    _____

    _____

    _____

SCIENCE EXTENSION

Choose five geologic time periods. Write the name of each time period at the top of each column. In the space below it, write the name of an organism that evolved during that time period. You can also draw the organism.

Challenge

PART A **Geologic Time Period Names**

The names of the different eons, eras, periods, and epochs of the geologic time scale come from different sources. Some are derived from Greek or Latin words. Others were named for the areas in which rocks of the time period were first studied. Use your textbook and independent research to match up the time spans below with the origins of their names.

_____ **1.** Cretaceous Period   _____ **6.** Mississippian Period

_____ **2.** Jurassic Period   _____ **7.** Devonian Period

_____ **3.** Triassic Period   _____ **8.** Silurian Period

_____ **4.** Permian Period   _____ **9.** Ordovician Period

_____ **5.** Pennsylvanian Period   _____ **10.** Cambrian Period

a. This period is named for discoveries made in Devonshire, England.

b. This period is named for the Jura Mountains near Switzerland.

c. White, chalky-looking cliffs along the English Channel are made of rocks from this period. This name came from the Latin word for chalk, _creta_.

d. This name came from the name of a Celtic tribe, the Ordovices.

e. This name came from the name of a Celtic tribe, the Silures.

f. This came from the Latin name for Wales, England, which was _Cambria_.

g. This period was named for Perm, Russia.

h. Rocks of this age are named for the large limestone cliffs that border the Mississippi River. A great number of rocks of this age are limestone.

i. Rocks of this age contain a lot of coal. They are particularly abundant in Pennsylvania.

j. This name comes from the Greek _trias_, which means three.

PART B   A Glimpse Into Past Life

Choose a geologic time period or epoch to do more research about. What did the land or shore look like? How was the weather? What sorts of living things were present then? Make a drawing to describe your findings. Draw the landscape or ocean, and include at least two plants and two animals that lived then. Research fossils and use them to decide what the living things may have looked like. Remember that a period could last millions of years—be sure that your chosen animals or plants were all alive at the same time. Share and explain your drawing to your classmates.

SCIENCE EXTENSION

Index Fossils and the Geologic Time Scale

As you learned in Chapter 11, index fossils are used for relative dating of rocks. These are fossils of organisms that lived during a certain time span. For example, trilobites lived only during the Paleozoic Era and can be used as an index fossil for certain time periods within this era. They do not occur in rocks that are younger than about 248 million years.

1. Choose two geologic time spans—eras, periods, or epochs. Do your own research to find an index fossil for each of these time spans. Write your results in a well-developed paragraph in your Science Notebook, and share your findings with the class.

2. Look through your textbook chapter. Which of the living things described do you think would *not* make good index fossils? Explain.

_____

_____

_____

_____

_____

_____

_____

_____

Key Concept Review

PART A   **Vocabulary**

Fill in the blanks below using the correct term. You will not use all of the terms.

air pressure	stratosphere	conduction
ozone	mesosphere	convection
troposphere	radiation	greenhouse effect

1. The number of molecules of gas decreases as altitude increases. The result is a drop in _____.

2. The layer of Earth's atmosphere closest to the ground is called the _____.

3. Air that comes in contact with Earth's surface absorbs heat through _____.

4. Atmospheric warming from gases is called the _____.

PART B   **Comprehension**

Read each of the questions about the atmosphere and answer them on the lines provided.

5. What must be equal for conditions on Earth to remain livable?

6. Explain the name of the thermosphere.

7. What creates wind?

8. Which gas makes up the largest part of Earth's atmosphere?

SCIENCE EXTENSION

The increase in greenhouse gases is affecting life on Earth in a negative way. Conduct research to learn how these gases absorb heat and slowly release it into the atmosphere, causing Earth to get increasingly warmer. Then write a paragraph describing some of the effects that global warming has had on our communities and our environment.

Vocabulary Review

PART A

Complete the table using new vocabulary terms from the chapter. Write an example of each term in the third column.

Term	Definition	Example
1.	the weight exerted on a specific area by the column of air above it	2.
atmosphere	3.	4.
5.	circular patterns caused by the rising and sinking of air	6.
7.	the deflection of the wind direction due to Earth's rotation	8.
greenhouse gases	9.	10.
wind	11.	12.

PART B

Draw a diagram relating these words: *radiation, convection,* and *conduction*. Include definitions of the words.

SCIENCE EXTENSION

Describe at least two characteristics of the following types of winds: trade winds, prevailing westerlies, polar easterlies, doldrums, horse latitudes, jet stream, valley breeze, and mountain breeze. Trade descriptions with a partner and identify the types of wind your partner has described.

Interpreting Diagrams

PART A

Label the diagram of Earth's atmosphere with the following: exosphere, ionosphere, mesosphere, ozone layer, tropopause, troposphere, stratosphere, and thermosphere.

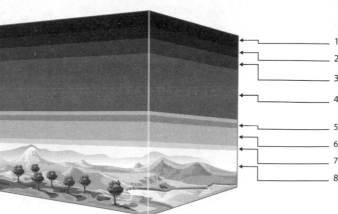

PART B

Place the letters of each description next to the appropriate layers on the diagram.

a. shields Earth from ultraviolet radiation

b. Satellites can orbit in this layer without much friction.

c. helps transmit radio signals around the world

d. coldest layer of the atmosphere

e. number of air molecules is very few in this layer

f. densest layer that contains most of the atmosphere's mass

g. absorbs great amounts of UV radiation

h. source of the aurora borealis

i. where most meteors burn up and appear as shooting stars

j. temperature may be more than 1000°C at the top of this layer

k. layer in which airplanes fly

l. Most of Earth's weather takes place in this layer.

SCIENCE EXTENSION

Conduct research to learn the name and purpose of a satellite currently in orbit around Earth. Write a paragraph describing the satellite's name, purpose, position in the atmosphere, speed of travel, and any other interesting information you can find.

Reading Comprehension

PART A **K-W-L-H Chart**

Although the atmosphere is invisible and its presence is hard to visualize, you would not live more than a few minutes without it. Besides giving us air to breathe, it has other important functions. As you read through Section 13.1, create a K-W-L-H chart on atmosphere in your Science Notebook. In the column labeled *K*, write what you know about our atmosphere. In the column labeled *W*, write what you want to learn about them. As you identify the information you want to find out about our atmosphere, write it in the *L* column. Finally, write how you can learn more about the atmosphere in the *H* column.

PART B **Vocabulary Webs**

The atmosphere is made up of layers that are based on temperature changes. Sometimes it is hard to remember which characteristics go with which layer. Create vocabulary webs for each layer, starting with the terms *troposphere, stratosphere, mesosphere, thermosphere,* and *exosphere.* Each web will connect the following characteristics to the correct layer. Some words or phrases may be used more than once. If needed, read Chapter 13 again.

meteors burn up here; densest layer; tropopause; auroras; blends into outer space; shooting stars; contains life forms; contains light gases; ionosphere; helps transmit radio signals; airplanes fly here; contains ozone; satellites orbit here; coldest part

SCIENCE EXTENSION

What's in a Title?

Carol is reading several books about the adventures of Wendy Windy, a fearless traveler. On separate index cards, she wrote the book title. On other index cards, she wrote a short description of what the book is about. She dropped all the cards and now needs to reorder them. Use the title of the book to decide which description matches that book. Draw a line from the title to the correct description.

Title:		Short Description:
1. *Doldrums and Horses*	a.	Each night when the sun sets, Wendy feels the warm afternoons change into cold nights.
2. *Riding the Jet Stream*	b.	Wendy takes an idea from history to use the westerlies to her advantage.
3. *Camping in the Mountains*	c.	Belts of low and high pressure circle the globe, stranding Wendy.
4. *The Breeze of the Seas*	d.	Wendy feels the pressure made by cold water during the day and by warm water at night.
5. *Sailing Back to Europe*	e.	Wendy notices that her kite flies in winds that curve to the right.
6. *Moved by the Coriolis Effect*	f.	Narrow belts of high-speed wind follow an irregular path, sending Wendy around the Earth.

History Connection: Sailing and Trade Routes

PART A

Before the advent of steamships—and long before airplanes—traders used large sailing ships to cross the oceans. They depended on the wind to take them to their destination. The map below shows the predominant winds that affected sailors: the northeast trade winds, the southeast trade winds, and the prevailing westerlies.

Next to each number, write the name of the corresponding wind system:

Map of world winds

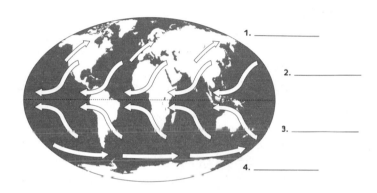

1. _____

2. _____

3. _____

4. _____

PART B

Think about these different types of winds and the areas that sailors wanted to avoid at the equator and 30 degrees north and south latitude. On the blank map below, draw a route that a sailor should take from Europe to the U.S. and back again in order to sail as quickly as possible.

SCIENCE EXTENSION

Determine from which direction the wind usually blows in your town or city during the winter and summer. Write this in your Science Notebook. Explain what factors cause the wind to blow from that direction in winter and then in summer.

Challenge Activity

PART A Life at High Altitudes

Take a look at the directions on packaged foods, such as pastas or cake mixes, in the grocery store. In the instructions, do any of them give special directions for "high-altitude preparation"?

Cooking and baking are slightly different for people living in the mountains compared to people who live near sea level. This is because of decreased air pressure at high altitudes. Research high-altitude cooking. Specifically, find out how boiling water is affected by altitude. Also, how might bread dough act differently at higher altitudes? Make a poster to describe your findings. On your poster, include a favorite recipe, with one version of the recipe for sea level and one for high altitude. Share your poster and recipes with your classmates.

PART B Wind Stories

Many ancient cultures have stories or myths to explain the origin of the Sun and stars and natural events, such as storms or earthquakes. There are also stories and legends about winds. Certain winds may have even been imagined to be controlled by particular gods. For example, in Greek mythology the god Zephyr was the god of the west wind.

Choose an ancient culture and do your own research to find out how wind was described. What were some common stories about wind? Does the wind described correspond to a global wind, such as the trade winds or prevailing westerlies? Write your findings in a well-organized paragraph that you can share with your class. Include an explanation of what is now understood to cause global winds.

SCIENCE EXTENSION

Local Winds and Geography

Local winds are affected by landmasses and bodies of water. Examine your city or town carefully. What nearby features could affect local wind movement? Describe them in a few sentences. Then choose a city anywhere in the world that you would like to visit. What is the geography around this city? Use this to predict where there will be areas of low pressure and high pressure during the day or at night. How will this affect local winds? What global winds will pass over this city? Write your predictions in a well-developed paragraph.

Chapter 14

Key Concept Review

PART A   Outlining

As you read, fill in the outline of the chapter below using the main headings and subheadings of each lesson.

14.1: _____   14.3: _____

     A. _____   A. _____

     B. _____   B. _____

     C. _____   C. _____

     D. _____   14.4: _____

     E. _____   A. _____

14.2: _____   B. _____

     A. _____   C. _____

     B. _____   D. _____

     C. _____

PART B   Vocabulary

Circle the term that best completes each sentence below.

1. Clouds are formed by the (evaporation, condensation, precipitation) of water vapor.

2. (Dew point, Saturation point, Relative humidity) is the amount of water vapor in the air compared to the maximum amount of water vapor that the air can hold.

3. The boundary that forms between air masses is called a (front, change, cloud).

4. A (thunderstorm, tornado, hurricane) is a violent, rotating column of air that is in contact with the ground.

SCIENCE EXTENSION

Meteorologists use many tools to predict the weather. Watch a weather report broadcast on television. List each tool from this chapter being used to explain weather predictions in the report. Then write a paragraph in your Science Notebook explaining how the meteorologist used each of these tools to explain their predictions and data.

Weather

Vocabulary Review

PART A

Decide whether each statement is true or false. If a statement is true, write *true* in the blank. If the statement is false, replace the underlined word with the letter of the word that makes it true.

a. anemometer	**e.** hurricane	**i.** lightning
b. cloud	**f.** isobars	**j.** storm surge
c. condensation	**g.** isopleths	**k.** thunderstorm
d. evaporation	**h.** isotherms	**l.** tornado

_____ **1.** Relative humidity can be determined by using a <u>hygrometer</u>.

_____ **2.** A <u>hurricane</u> forms when warm, moist air rises in the atmosphere and cools. It is a collection of millions of tiny water droplets.

_____ **3.** <u>Isotherms</u> are lines of equal temperature on a weather map.

_____ **4.** A <u>barometer</u> is used to measure wind speed.

_____ **5.** In the water cycle, <u>evaporation</u> occurs as water vapor rises in the atmosphere, begins to cool, and then changes back into liquid water.

_____ **6.** A <u>tornado</u> occurs when winds drive ocean water toward coastal areas, where it washes over the land.

PART B

Review the new vocabulary in Lesson 14.1. Then complete the diagram using four new terms from the lesson. Give the definitions of two of the words.

7. _____ the amount of water vapor in the air	**8.** _____ ratio of the amount of water vapor in a specific amount of air to the maximum water vapor that amount of air can hold	reaches 100%

9. _____

10. _____

SCIENCE EXTENSION

Write a short article for a newspaper on the techniques a meteorologist uses to predict weather. Use at least three new vocabulary words from Lesson 14.4.

Interpreting Diagrams

PART A

Label the diagram by placing the appropriate letter of the air mass in the circles: A, cP, cT, mP, or mT. Write the meaning of the letters in the key next to the diagram.

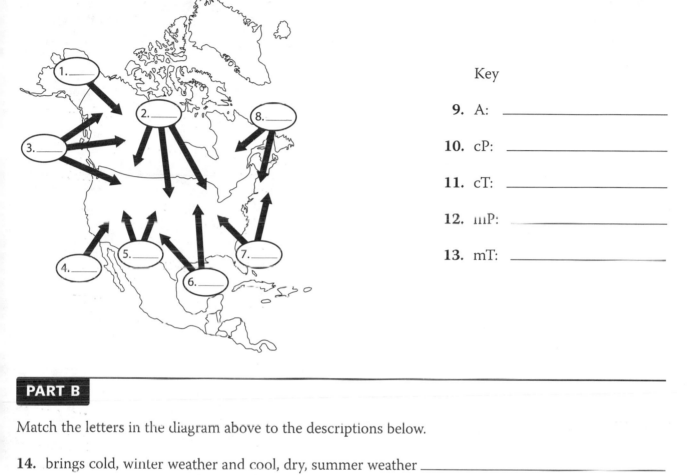

Key

9. A: _____

10. cP: _____

11. cT: _____

12. mP: _____

13. mT: _____

PART B

Match the letters in the diagram above to the descriptions below.

14. brings cold, winter weather and cool, dry, summer weather _____

15. brings hot, humid, summer weather and mild, cloudy, winter weather _____

16. brings snow, rain, cloudy, winter weather and cool, foggy, summer weather _____

17. brings clear, hot, dry, summer weather _____

Write the type of front in the blank next to the description.

_____ **18.** warm air moves over cold air; can bring cloudiness and drizzly rain; after front passes, weather is usually warm and clear

_____ **19.** cold air moves under warm air; can produce clouds, thunderstorms, heavy rain or snow; after front passes, weather is cooler

Reading Comprehension

PART A | Making Predictions

Examine each of the situations listed in the *Cause* column below. Match the responses
in the *Effect* column by drawing a line between them. Finally, draw a line connecting
the process that best describes each cause and effect.

Cause	Effect	Process
1. Sun heats up the surface of the water.	Water drops form clouds in solid or liquid form.	evaporation
2. Water vapor rises in the atmosphere.	Water changes from a liquid to a gas.	condensation
3. Water droplets combine.	Water changes from a gas to a liquid.	precipitation

PART B

Watching the changing skies can make for an entertaining afternoon. Clouds can take
many shapes and often remind us of people or familiar objects. Imagine that an art
studio decides to have an art show of drawings of clouds. Use the characteristics of
each type of cloud to make drawings in your Science Notebook. Pick a specific type of
cloud. Be sure that the drawing highlights its characteristics. Also, try to incorporate a
familiar image that you might see in a cloud. For instance, the drawing of a cumulus
cloud might include the profile of a man's face.

SCIENCE EXTENSION

Severe Weather Safety Tips
Meteorologists often tell people what they might experience during a threatening
storm and how to stay safe. To which type of storm—*tornado, hurricane,* or *thunder
and lightning storm*—does each of the following refer?

a. "We expect the wind to blow at 120 mph. Torrential rains and flooding are expected.
Stay away from low-lying areas. Stay indoors because the strong winds will blow things
around. If you live in a mobile home or a flood-prone area, go immediately to a shelter.
If your emergency personnel say to evacuate, then do so immediately." _____

b. "If you see the sky get dark and hear a load roar, go to your basement. If you do
not have a basement, go to an interior room without windows such as a bathroom
or closet. If you can, get under a sturdy piece of furniture like a table. If you live in a
mobile home, get out of it; if you are driving, get out of your car. Go to a ditch or
low-lying area and lie flat in it. Stay away from fallen power lines and stay out of damaged
areas." _____

Chapter 14

Physics Connection: Lightning and Static Electricity

PART A

Lightning is an example of static electricity. Matter is made up of atoms. Atoms have positively charged particles called protons and negatively charged particles called electrons. Opposite charges attract, and like charges repel each other. When you walk across a carpet in socks, you accumulate electrons. When you touch a metal doorknob, which contains more protons, there is an exchange of electrons, a charge builds up, and you get a shock.

1. How is a lightning strike similar to the shock you get when you touch a doorknob?

   _____

2. In the diagrams below, draw the positive and negative charges before a lightning strike (A), and during a lightning strike (B).

   A.   B.

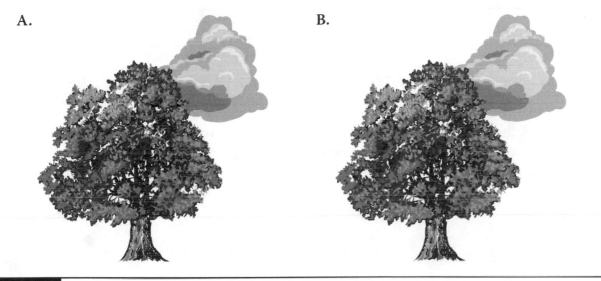

PART B

Using the information you have learned, fill in the blanks below with the correct term.

3. Opposite charges _____. Like charges _____. Protons carry a _____ charge. Electrons carry a _____ charge. When lightning strikes, there is an _____ between the clouds and the ground.

SCIENCE EXTENSION

During a storm, negative charges may accumulate in tall objects such as mountains, trees, or even people. Lightning is more likely to strike these objects. Water and metal are good conductors of electricity, and, if lightning strikes, it will send the current through a person touching them. Given these things, if you are standing by a lake with tall trees and metal canoes nearby, what should you do if you are far from shelter and lightning is in the area? What shouldn't you do? Write an explanation in your Science Notebook.

Challenge Activity

PART A   Careers in Meteorology

There are many career options for someone who studies meteorology. A meteorologist might be a researcher for private companies or the government, a teacher, or a weather forecaster on television. What type of education does someone need to become a meteorologist? A college degree in atmospheric studies or meteorology is a good start.

1. Do your own research to find a school that offers a degree in atmospheric studies or meteorology. Find out more about the program and make a list of the classes that students must take to earn their degrees. For two of these classes, predict why a meteorologist would need to learn the information taught.

    _____

    _____

    _____

    _____

2. Next, imagine that you have the chance to speak to a meteorologist. What would you ask that person about his or her job? Make a list of 10 questions to ask this person. If you have the opportunity, interview a meteorologist using these questions.

    _____

    _____

    _____

    _____

    _____

    _____

    _____

    _____

PART B **Official Hurricane Names**

Each year, individual tropical storms (hurricanes and cyclones) are given names. The name lists are chosen several years in advance. Using these names makes it easy to educate and warn the public about upcoming storms.

3. Choose a year anywhere from 1950–2010. Do your own research to find out which names were chosen for hurricanes forming in the Gulf of Mexico/Caribbean Sea/North Atlantic Ocean. How many names are/were chosen? What do you notice about these names?

_____

_____

_____

SCIENCE EXTENSION

Preparing for Severe Weather

Severe weather can occur everywhere in the United States. Which type of severe weather are you most at risk for where you live? Is your family prepared in case of a severe storm? Write up a plan for how to deal with a major storm. Include information about how you will know if a storm is coming. For example, will there be warning sirens for a tornado? What information might come over television or radio? Make a list of supplies you might need if you lose power. Also think about what might happen if your family is separated. How will you contact each other or leave messages for one another? Where can you get help if you need it?

_____

_____

_____

_____

_____

_____

_____

_____

Key Concept Review

Climate

Chapter 15

PART A Classify

On a separate sheet of paper, draw a concept map using the six titles from the Koeppen classification system: *Tropical, Dry, Mild, Continental, Polar,* and *High Elevation.* Then classify each term or phrase below by writing it under the appropriate title.

year-round high temperatures	influenced by oceans	desert
arid	high latitudes	steppe
marine west coast	Mediterranean	humid subtropical
semiarid	interior of continents	coldest regions
rain forests	savanna	mountaintops

PART B Comprehension

Read each of the questions below and answer them on the lines provided. Use a separate piece of paper if necessary.

1. What is the difference between weather and climate? _____

_____

2. Compare the tropics to polar zones and temperate zones. _____

_____

3. Which climates are cooler: mountain climates or climates at sea level? Why?

_____

4. Are seasonal changes in climate considered long-term climatic changes or short-term climatic changes? _____

_____

5. How do humans contribute to global warming? _____

_____

SCIENCE EXTENSION

Global warming can result in severe consequences. Research and describe an area of the world whose climate has been negatively affected by global warming. Then explain what human behaviors might be changed to stop these negative effects from continuing to occur.

Vocabulary Review

PART A

Match the following definitions to one of the words in the list below. Write the letter
of the definition in the blank next to the word.

1. _____ deforestation   4. _____ interglacial interval   7. _____ savanna

2. _____ elliptical   5. _____ leeward   8. _____ steppe

3. _____ heat island   6. _____ microclimate   9. _____ temperate zone

a. land areas made up of tall grasses and scattered trees

b. the oval pattern that Earth's orbit sometimes takes around the Sun

c. the side of a mountain on which the air has lost its moisture and is now dry

d. semiarid region that receives slightly more rainfall than deserts

e. zones which lie between 23.5 and 66.5 degrees north or south of the equator

f. city area that has a warmer climate than the surrounding rural area

g. small area with a climate different from the climate of the larger region that
surrounds it

h. cutting down of forests

i. a warmer period of time that alternates with an ice age

PART B

Review new vocabulary from Lessons 15.1 and 15.2. Then complete the diagram
using some of the words from the lessons.

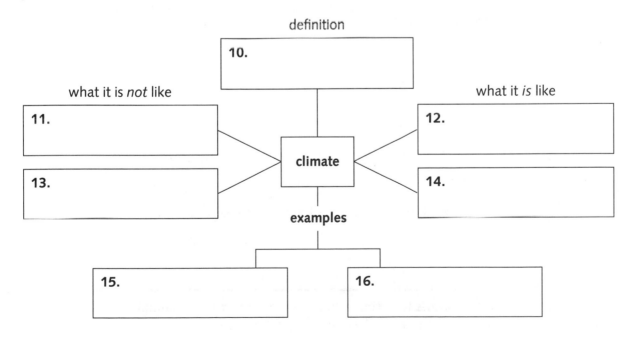

Graphic Organizer

PART A

Complete the chart of Earth's climate types.

Type of Climate	Location	Precipitation and Temperature
Tropical: wet	1.	2.
3. Tropical: _____	4.	dry winters, warm year-round
Dry: arid	5.	6.
7.	steppes, at higher latitudes than deserts	8.
Mild: humid subtropical marine	9.	10.
11. Mild: _____	12.	year-round rainfall, cool summers, mild winters
13. Mild: _____	14.	15.
16.	17.	temperature swings, cold winters; warm, wet summers
18.	high latitudes in northern and southern hemispheres	19.
Localized	20.	21.

PART B

Fill in the blanks with one of the following letters to describe a factor that affects climate: *L* for latitude, *T* for topography, *P* for prevailing winds, or *O* for ocean currents.

_____ **22.** Mountain areas tend to be cooler than areas at sea level.

_____ **23.** Coastal areas are cooler than inland areas.

_____ **24.** Regions close to the equator are warmer than regions close to the poles.

_____ **25.** Regions close to large lakes tend to get lake-effect snow.

SCIENCE EXTENSION

Draw a sequence diagram that shows the effects on climate of one of these natural events: ice age, solar activity, El Niño, volcanic eruption, Earth's tilt, Earth's orbit, or Earth's wobble.

Reading Comprehension

PART A **Where Should I Live?**

After reading the following descriptions of the kind of weather each person enjoys, decide if each should live on the windward or leeward side of a mountain and why.

1. Jen: "I enjoy spending my time indoors and I really do not like it when it is hot out. I love listening to the rain on my roof and watching storms roll in." _____

    _____

2. Andrew: "I just want to be outside. I want to hike and bike and run—I think I would live outside if I could." _____

    _____

PART B **What Kind of Climate?**

Lesson 15.2 discusses the many different climates on Earth and how they are classified. Answer the following questions about what you have read.

3. In which type of climate would you most likely find a savanna? _____

4. If an area's warm season's highest temperature is less than 10°C, what kind of climate would it be classified as? _____

5. What type of climate does most of the southeastern United States have? _____

6. A city experiencing higher temperatures than its surrounding area and a mountain top with a lower temperature than the lower-elevation areas surrounding are examples of what? _____

7. In what climate would you most likely find steppes? _____

SCIENCE EXTENSION

Is it hot in here, or is it just global warming?

Despite much debate about what is causing global warming, there is no arguing the fact that it is happening, and it is having a negative impact on Earth. Below is a list of contributors to global warming. On a separate sheet of paper, list some things that can help combat their effect on global warming.

a. burning fossil fuels, such as oil, coal, and natural gas

b. automobile emissions from burning gasoline

c. deforestation, or cutting down forests

Culture Connection: The Inuit

PART A

The climate in which people live greatly affects their lifestyles and their cultures. The Inuit live in the Arctic, north of the timberline, where few or no trees grow. They have traditionally depended on the plants and animals of the tundra, lakes, rivers, and ocean for their food, shelter, and clothing. Use your knowledge of the Arctic climate to answer the following questions.

1. Before they could buy food, how would the Inuit have acquired most of their food?

_____

2. What do you think the staples of their diet were?

_____

3. What building materials would they have had available for their homes?

_____

PART B

Think about what you would need in order to survive and be comfortable if you were planning to spend a year living in the Arctic. List five of the most important things you would choose to bring with you.

_____

_____

_____

SCIENCE EXTENSION

Global warming has been causing big changes in the Arctic. There is less sea ice in the summer, and it is forming later and melting earlier. Areas of permafrost are melting, causing buildings and roads to sink. Some entire towns have had to move to more stable areas. These changes are also affecting plant and animal life. What effect do you think warmer temperatures are having on plants and animals? On a separate sheet of paper, list three possible changes that could be occurring.

Challenge Activity

PART A Plant Growth in Different Climates

1. Plant life varies from climate to climate. Vegetation that grows in one area will not grow well in an area with a different climate. Choose one of the six climate types in Koeppen's classification system, or choose a climate subtype. Conduct research to determine the type of plants that live in this climate. Make a poster to display information about two or three of these plants. On the poster, include details about the climate. What are the average minimum and maximum temperatures for each season? How much rainfall is there each year?

2. Imagine you want to plant an outdoor garden. Choose three fruits or vegetables you would like to plant, and do research to find out the conditions they need to grow. Based on your area's climate, would these plants grow well if you did not water them or protect them from the Sun? If they would succeed in your climate, what time of year should you plant them? Write your findings in a few well-formed sentences.

PART B Carbon Dioxide and Gasoline-Powered Engines

Gasoline is used to power many machines and vehicles. It is estimated that 19 pounds of carbon dioxide are released for every gallon of gasoline burned. How much carbon dioxide do you release into the atmosphere every year because of burning gasoline? You can make an estimate using the following method.

3. Make a list of all of the vehicles or machines you use that burn gasoline.

_____

_____

4. Determine how much gasoline each machine (other than a car or bus) burns for each use. For example, how many gallons of gasoline does it take to mow a lawn? If you do not have an exact number, make an estimate.

_____

_____

Estimate how many times you use a particular machine per year: _____

Estimate how much gasoline you burn each year with this machine: _____

Repeat these steps for all machines. Total gasoline burned each year (machines) = _____

5. Determine about how much gasoline the main car you ride in burns for every mile of travel. You can use the library or the Internet to find this information.

Estimate how many miles you ride or drive each week: _____

Use this number to determine how much gasoline is burned: _____

Divide the gasoline burned each week by the average number of people that ride in the car. For example, if 4 people ride in a car that burns 2 gallons/week, each person uses 0.5 gallons/week:

_____

Multiply the gasoline you burn each week by 52 to find out the amount of gasoline burned in a year. Total gasoline burned each year (car) = _____

6. Find out if the bus you ride uses gasoline, or another fuel (like a fuel called natural gas). If it runs on gasoline, assume that it uses about 3 gallons for every mile.

Estimate how many miles you ride on the bus each week: _____

Use this number to determine how much gasoline is burned each week: _____

Divide the gasoline burned each week by the average number of people that ride the bus the same time that you do: _____. This is the amount of gasoline you burn each week by riding the bus.

Multiply the gasoline you burn each week by 52 to find out the amount of gasoline burned in a year. Total gasoline burned each year (bus) = _____

7. Add the gallons of gasoline burned each year from machines, car, and bus. _____

Multiply this by 19 to find the amount of CO_2 sent into the atmosphere every year. _____

8. How do you think your gasoline use compares to that of other people in the United States? Explain your answer. _____

9. If every person in the United States used the same amount of gasoline as you use, how much CO_2 would be released every year? _____

10. If the number of miles that your car or bus could travel on one gallon of gas was doubled, how would the CO_2 you released from burning gasoline change in one year?

_____

_____

_____

Key Concept Review

PART A Vocabulary

Answer each question below using the correct term from the list. You will not use all of the terms.

channel	delta	irrigation	bog
tributary	levee	swamp	porosity
watershed	eutrophication	marsh	permeability

1. A _____ is a sloping pathway in which water flows.

2. A _____ is a high ridge usually made of soil and other natural materials, built along a riverbank.

3. _____ is the process by which a lake becomes overly rich in nutrients that are washed in from the surrounding watershed.

4. A _____ is an area of soaked, spongy soil that may not be covered in standing water.

5. _____ is the ability of a material to let water pass through it.

PART B Comprehension

Answer each of the questions about water. Use a separate sheet of paper if necessary.

6. What determines the size of particles that a stream can carry?

_____

7. How does a meander form?

_____

8. How can flooding be useful?

_____

9. What is the effect of eutrophication?

_____

SCIENCE EXTENSION

Each type of freshwater environment provides a different kind of habitat for wildlife. Choose two types of freshwater habitats. Compare and contrast their features; describe their freshwater supply and how it impacts the wildlife it supports.

Vocabulary Review

PART A

Fill in the blanks using terms from the list below:

aquifer	divide	lake	spring
cave	spring	levee	swamp
channel	estuary	marsh	well
delta	geyser	runoff	wetland

1. high land area separating one watershed from another _____

2. brackish body of water that forms where a river enters an ocean _____

3. deep hole dug or drilled to reach the water table _____

4. triangular-shaped deposit in water made of silt and clay _____

5. water that flows over the ground rather than soaking into it _____

6. land area covered with water for a large part of the year _____

7. wetland that supports trees, shrubs, or other woody plants _____

8. shoots steam and water vapor into air from underground reservoirs _____

9. natural opening in ground through which groundwater flows _____

PART B

Write a well-developed paragraph using the following vocabulary terms:

alluvial fan	recharge
bog	reservoir
eutrophication	sinkhole
floodplains	watershed
permeability	water table
porosity	

SCIENCE EXTENSION

Draw an illustration that shows either the various types of wetlands or groundwater and how it collects underground. Label the illustration with new vocabulary terms and their definitions.

Interpreting Diagrams

PART A

Label the diagram of the river system using these words: *delta, estuary, meander, oxbow lake, river, meltwater,* and *tributary.* Then write the letter of the correct description next to each label.

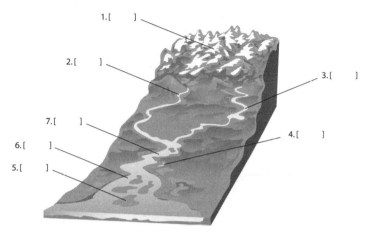

1.[   ]
2.[   ]
3.[   ]
4.[   ]
5.[   ]
6.[   ]
7.[   ]

a. a smaller river that flows into a larger river

b. where freshwater and saltwater meet

c. forms in a C-shaped section from a walled-off meander

d. a bend or curve in a river channel

e. rainfall or melting snow that flows downhill in channels

f. a triangular-shaped deposit where a river and a large body of water meet

g. a wider, deeper, longer version of a stream

PART B

Place a check in the column that matches the description.

Description	Wetlands	Lake	Groundwater
8. One type forms in flat, low-lying areas along streams.			
9. Aquifers collect and store the water.			
10. many formed from the actions of glaciers			
11. act as natural reservoirs that store and hold water			
12. causes the weathering and erosion that form caves			

SCIENCE EXTENSION

Draw an illustration of two streams with different gradients, discharges, and loads. Then write a paragraph comparing and contrasting the erosion and deposition of the two streams.

Reading Comprehension

PART A   How did that happen?

Freshwater affects the formation of features that are present all around the world. Explain in your own words how freshwater affects how these features are formed. Refer to Chapter 16 as needed.

1. channels _____

_____

2. oxbow lakes _____

_____

3. deltas _____

_____

4. sinkhole _____

_____

PART B   Comprehension

Explain how the terms listed below are related. Refer to Chapter 16 for help.

5. *water cycle* and *evaporation* _____

_____

6. *runoff* and *hills* _____

_____

7. *irrigation* and *crops* _____

_____

8. *deposition* and *sediment* _____

_____

9. *eutrophication* and *algae* _____

_____

10. *alluvial fan* and *sand and gravel* _____

_____

Music Connection: The Delta Blues

PART A

The Mississippi Delta is the flood plain of the lower Mississippi River. It was originally a swampy wilderness inhabited by a number of Native American groups. However, it contained very fertile soil, and settlers who came drained part of it and turned it into productive farmland. Huge agricultural plantations dominated the landscape, and plantation owners used mostly enslaved African Americans to raise cotton and other crops. These slaves and their descendants, who were often poor tenant farmers called sharecroppers, expressed the difficulty and unhappiness of their lives in a unique form of music called the blues. Sharecroppers were very poor and also had few rights because of the laws and attitudes of the time. Many of them migrated north up the river to Chicago, and then to other cities like New York and Detroit. They brought the blues with them, and the blues influenced other music. Jazz, soul, rock and roll, rap, and hip-hop all incorporated the sounds of the Delta blues. Read the lyrics to the song "I's Be Troubled" written by Muddy Waters. Then answer the questions that follow.

Well if I feel tomorrow
Like I feel today
I'm gonna pack my suitcase
And make my getaway
Lord I'm troubled, I'm all worried in mind
And I'm never bein' satisfied,
And I just can't keep from cryin'

1. Look at a United States map. What states are included in the region of the Mississippi Delta?

2. Why would sharecroppers have had difficult lives?

3. What is the narrator of this song planning on doing?

4. Why do you think people wanted to write and sing about having the "blues"?

SCIENCE EXTENSION

Super Soil

Use what you have learned about rivers to explain in your Science Notebook why the Mississippi Delta has such fertile soil.

Challenge Activity

PART A   Rivers and Industry

Throughout history, many industries have been built around rivers. These include industries, such as mills and power plants, that use the energy of the moving water. Rivers have also been commonly used for transportation.

1. Do your own research about a river in your state. Write an essay about the history of industry on this river. What did people first use the river for? Are any of the industries from the past still running today? Include information about how the cities and towns along the river are affected by river industries today. For example, do they depend on these industries for jobs and money? Have they developed new businesses that do not rely on the river? Or perhaps both? Use the space below for notes.

_____

_____

_____

_____

_____

_____

_____

_____

_____

_____

_____

_____

_____

_____

PART B Freshwater Extremes

Some noteworthy bodies of water are listed below. Match each with its description. Then, choose one of these on which to do more research and answer the following questions: What are some large cities in the region of this water? What kinds of plants and animals live in or near the water? Is the water threatened by pollution or over-use? Write your findings in three or four well-formed sentences.

2.   Lake Superior _____

3.   Lake Baikal _____

4.   Amazon River _____

5.   High plains aquifer _____

6.   Nile River _____

7.   Yellowstone Lake _____

8.   Crater Lake _____

a.   This is the deepest freshwater lake in the world.

b.   Hippopotamuses live in what is perhaps the world's longest river.

c.   This South American river carries more water than any of Earth's other rivers.

d.   This is the largest lake in the United States, at an elevation of 7,000 feet.

e.   This is the largest freshwater lake in the world.

f.   With a maximum depth of around 590 meters (around 1,950 feet), this is the deepest lake in the United States.

g.   This water source underlies parts of eight midwestern and Western states in the U.S.

Key Concept Review

PART A Outlining

As you read, fill in the outline of the chapter below using the main headings and subheadings of each lesson.

17.1: _____

    A. _____

    B. _____

    C. _____

    D. _____

    E. _____

    F. _____

    G. _____

17.2: _____

    A. _____

    B. _____

    C. _____

    D. _____

    E. _____

17.3: _____

    A. _____

    B. _____

    C. _____

    D. _____

    E. _____

    F. _____

    G. _____

    H. _____

    I. _____

    J. _____

    K. _____

    L. _____

    M. _____

    N. _____

PART B Vocabulary

Circle the term that best completes each sentence below.

1. (Radar, Sonar, Scuba) uses sound waves to detect and measure objects underwater.

2. The (salinity, temperature profile, density) of ocean water is a measure of its concentration of dissolved salts.

3. A (surface current, density current, wavelength) is a wind-driven movement of ocean water that affects the upper few hundred meters of the ocean.

Vocabulary Review

PART A

Match each term in Column B with its description in Column A. Write the letter of the correct term in the space provided.

Column A

1. _____ huge ocean wave caused by a major disturbance to ocean floor

2. _____ strong tide during new moon or full moon

3. _____ upward movement of ocean water

4. _____ forms when ocean waters with different temperatures and salinities meet

5. _____ a measure of the concentration of dissolved salts in the ocean

6. _____ weak tide during first-quarter or third-quarter moon phases

7. _____ large mass of floating ice

8. _____ periodic rise and fall of sea level

9. _____ an effect of Earth's rotation on its axis

10. _____ a closed, circular current system, affected by continents

11. _____ height of the surfaces of the oceans

Column B

a. Coriolis effect

b. density current

c. gyre

d. iceberg

e. neap tide

f. salinity

g. sea level

h. spring tide

i. tide

j. tsunami

k. upwelling

PART B

Label the following parts of the diagram with these words and their definitions: *breaker, crest, trough, wave,* and *wavelength.*

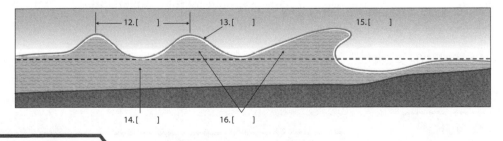

12.[   ]   13.[   ]   15.[   ]

14.[   ]   16.[   ]

SCIENCE EXTENSION

Write a short paragraph about the science of oceanography. Describe at least two fields of study, the technology used in these fields, and one recent discovery in each of the fields.

Interpreting Diagrams

PART A

Label the three ocean layers in the diagram below. Then write the letters of the descriptions that apply to each layer.

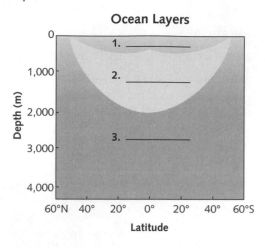

Ocean Layers

1. _____

2. _____

3. _____

Depth (m): 0, 1,000, 2,000, 3,000, 4,000

Latitude: 60°N 40° 20° 0° 20° 40° 60°S

a. Temperature ranges from about −2°C at the poles to 30°C at the equator.

b. Temperature stays just above the freezing point of water.

c. Layer is deepest at the equator and gradually becomes less deep at higher latitudes.

d. Only low light reaches this layer.

e. Photosynthesis takes place in this layer.

f. Layer does not exist at the poles.

g. This is the layer with the greatest density.

PART B

Complete the following statements.

4. Earth's three major oceans in order from largest to smallest are _____.

5. The climates of cities next to the ocean are more moderate than inland cities because _____.

6. Three factors that affect surface currents are _____

_____.

SCIENCE EXTENSION

Write a short entry for a geographical dictionary on ocean salinity. Include factors that affect the salinity of oceans. List at least two geographical places or regions where each of these factors might be present.

Reading Comprehension

PART A

A classmate has asked you to go over this chapter with her. She asks you the following questions. Write your answers below. Refer to Chapter 17 for help.

1. My grandparents live in Ohio; how does the ocean affect their weather?

    _____

    _____

2. If water moves in a continuous cycle, evaporating and condensing, how did it first get here?

    _____

    _____

3. If living things need light and oxygen to survive, how can there be life on the bottom of the ocean?

    _____

    _____

PART B   **Water Movement**

Ocean water is constantly moving and circulating. Refer to Lesson 17.3 to help you answer the following questions.

4. How do gyres help even out Earth's temperature differences? _____

    _____

5. How does upwelling change the water in the ocean? _____

    _____

6. Why would a density current form at the poles? _____

    _____

SCIENCE EXTENSION

Time Travel

You are vacationing in London and enjoying its warm temperatures and mild weather. You are offered an opportunity to travel to London's future. This seems intriguing, so you agree. When you arrive in futuristic London, it is freezing. There is snow and ice on the ground. When you ask people why it is so cold, they give you funny looks and tell you it is always this cold. On a separate sheet of paper, describe what factors could have caused this drastic change in London's climate.

Chemistry Connection: Salinity

PART A

Salinity varies in different parts of Earth's oceans. Use the map of ocean salinity below to answer the questions that follow.

Surface Salinities of the Oceans

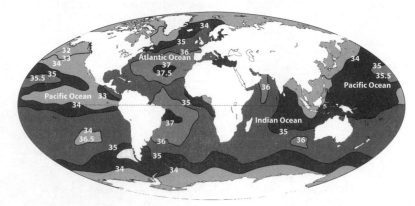

1. What are three areas that have the highest salinity? Why do you think that they have higher salinity?

_____

_____

2. What areas have the lowest salinity? Explain.

_____

PART B

The average salinity of ocean water is 35 parts per thousand (ppt). Freshwater has a salinity level between 0 and 5 ppt. Brackish water, such as that in estuaries, varies between 5 and 35 ppt, with lower levels closer to freshwater rivers and higher levels closer to oceans. In the map of an estuary at the right, write possible salinity levels at the four locations marked.

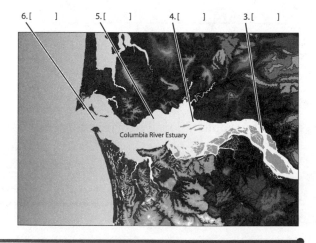

Columbia River Estuary

SCIENCE EXTENSION

Diffusion Solution

Water passes across animal membranes from areas of lower salinity to areas of higher salinity. Some marine organisms prevent water loss from their bodies by having the same salinity level in their bodies as there is in the ocean. Use this fact to explain why crabs and shrimp often taste salty.

Challenge Activity

PART A **Crossword Puzzle**

The crossword puzzle below contains words and information about oceans. Use the clues and your own research to fill in the crossword.

ACROSS

4. Light that hits ocean waters is absorbed, transmitted, or _____.

6. Most icebergs in the North Atlantic Ocean have broken off of glaciers in _____.

9. Wind drives this type of ocean current.

11. Bacteria that live near hot springs on the ocean floor do not need this to survive.

12. Cold water is _____ dense than warm water.

13. The name of an ocean-monitoring satellite came from the Greek god of the sea.

14. These bodies of seawater on rocky shorelines support a wide variety of life. They are exposed during low tide and are covered during high tide.

15. Ocean salinity is 3.7 percent in the _____.

DOWN

1. The Suez Canal connects the Mediterranean Sea to this sea.

2. This waterway separates Alaska and Russia and connects the Arctic and Pacific oceans.

3. This ocean animal is the largest animal living on the planet.

5. These small icebergs are more dangerous to ships than large icebergs because they can be hidden by waves.

7. Gyres in the southern hemisphere circulate in this direction.

8. _____ contain up to 0.5 percent water.

9. This sea is not surrounded by land. It is part of the Atlantic Ocean and is surrounded by currents including the Gulf Stream and the North Atlantic Current. The algae Sargassum grows well in this sea.

10. The name of this type of wave is a Japanese word meaning "harbor wave."

PART B **Make Your Own Crossword**

Use the terms below to make your own crossword puzzle. Write the clues and draw the board. When you are finished, have your friends try to solve the puzzle.

<u>Word list:</u>

Baltic Sea
deep ocean currents
zooplankton
neap tide
Indian Ocean

thermocline
breaker
submersible
bay
gulf

Key Concept Review

PART A Sequencing

Number the following ocean life zones in the benthic environment in the
correct order, starting with the shallowest and continuing to the deepest.
On the second blank, name one creature from that zone.

_____ _____ Hadal Zone

_____ _____ Sublittoral Zone

_____ _____ Bathyl Zone

_____ _____ Intertidal Zone

_____ _____ Abyssal Zone

PART B Comprehension

Read and answer each of the questions about the marine environment.
Use an additional sheet of paper if necessary.

1. What is the difference between the continental shelf and the continental slope?

   _____

2. What are the deepest parts of the ocean basins called? Where are they especially
   common?

   _____

3. Name the three groups of marine life, and list some organisms that are included in each.

   _____

4. What are the possible causes for dead zones in coral reefs?

   _____

SCIENCE EXTENSION

Many changes in the ocean reflect human behaviors, not all of them good.
Choose one negative change that has occurred as a result of human behavior,
and write a paragraph describing how the behavior has caused this change.
Then write another paragraph describing how this change might be stopped or
reversed by changing human behavior.

Vocabulary Review

PART A

Match the following definitions to one of the terms in the list below. Write the letter of the definition in the blank next to the term.

1. _____ benthic environment

4. _____ habitat

7. _____ pelagic environment

2. _____ coral bleaching

5. _____ oceanic zone

8. _____ seamount

3. _____ dead zone

6. _____ overfishing

9. _____ turbidity current

a. includes all of the water that covers the sea floor except for the continental shelf

b. region where oxygen levels in the water are so low that the water cannot support large populations of organisms

c. all of the water in the ocean, and the marine organisms that live above the ocean floor

d. whitening of coral colonies due to the death of the algae that live within healthy corals

e. a rapidly flowing, deep-water current that carries a heavy load of sediment

f. the natural conditions and environment in which an organism lives

g. an underwater volcanic mountain at least one kilometer high

h. the ocean floor and all the organisms that live on or in it

i. occurs when too many fish or other marine animals are harvested

PART B

Identify the following in the diagram: *benthos, nekton,* and *plankton.* On your own paper, include definitions and examples for each word.

SCIENCE EXTENSION

Describe two or three features in two of the ocean life zones. Trade descriptions with a partner and identify the zones.

Interpreting Diagrams

PART A

Place the letters of the features shown below next to the correct term.

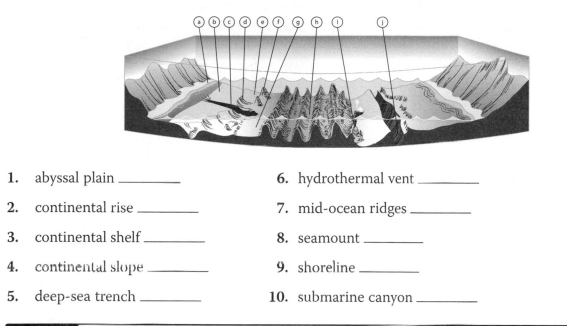

1. abyssal plain _____

2. continental rise _____

3. continental shelf _____

4. continental slope _____

5. deep-sea trench _____

6. hydrothermal vent _____

7. mid-ocean ridges _____

8. seamount _____

9. shoreline _____

10. submarine canyon _____

PART B

Write the name of the ocean life zone in the blank next to its description.

_____ 11. Water depth is from 400 meters to about 4,000 meters. Few plants live here. Animals include sponges and octopi.

_____ 12. This zone transforms with the tides twice daily. Clams, mussels, starfish, and anemones live here.

_____ 13. No plants live here. Animals include sea cucumbers, worms, and communities that live around hydrothermal vents.

_____ 14. Temperature, water pressure, and sunlight are fairly constant. Kelp forests and coral live here.

_____ 15. the zone with the greatest pressure; animals here include sponges, worms, and clams

_____ 16. the zone with the largest concentration of sea life

SCIENCE EXTENSION

Write a flyer that alerts members of your community to one change that is occurring in today's oceans. Describe the change and explain its effects. Then make a list of at least three actions members in the community can take to help oceans recover from this change.

Reading Comprehension

PART A | Summarizing

You have been asked to label a picture of the different characteristics of the ocean floor. The picture shows six characteristics for you to name: continental margin, continental shelf, continental slope, submarine canyon, abyssal plains, and mid-ocean ridges. In your Science Notebook, write a summary of each of these terms, including what they look like and, if you can, how they are formed. Refer to Chapter 18 if needed.

PART B | Where Do I Live?

Chapter 18 discusses the vast environment in the ocean. There are many organisms that are well-adapted for the environment in which they live. Based on the description of the habitat and the animals that live there, figure out whether they live in the *benthic* or *pelagic* environment, and then name the ecological zone they inhabit. Refer to Lesson 18.2 for help.

1. I am a starfish that holds on to rock faces. Sometimes I live in the water, and sometimes I live on land. _____

2. I am a sponge that lives 3,000 meters below the surface. I am well-adapted for a dark environment. _____

3. I am a fish that lives in plenty of sunlight. There is abundant food for me to eat, and the water is comfortably warm. _____

4. I am an anglerfish. I live in cold, dark, deep water. _____

5. I am a clam that lives in a deep ocean trench. I have never seen daylight, and the water is very cold. _____

6. I am a sea cucumber that lives 5,000 meters below the surface. I live near a hydrothermal vent. _____

7. I am a polyp living in a coral reef. There is sunlight, and lots of fish are swimming around. _____

SCIENCE EXTENSION

What Would You Do?

You are a scientist studying the problems facing Earth's oceans. Some of these problems are a result of naturally occurring events. However, the three problems listed below stem from the ignorance and neglect of humans. On a separate sheet of paper, give some examples of what you would do to help eliminate these problems.

Coral bleaching   Overfishing   Dead zones

Economics Connection: The Economics of Overfishing

Chapter 18

PART A

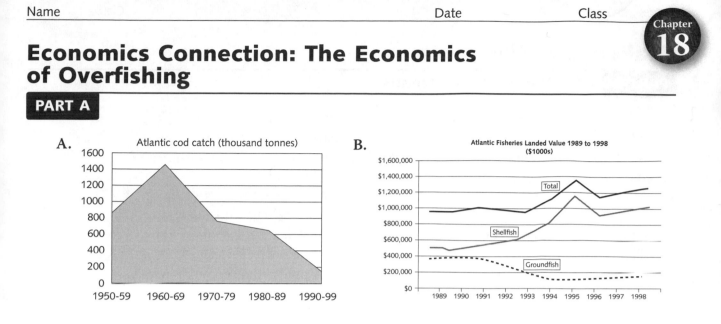

A. Atlantic cod catch (thousand tonnes)

B. Atlantic Fisheries Landed Value 1989 to 1998 ($1000s)

Use the information from graphs A and B to answer the following questions.

1. What happened to the Atlantic cod catch from 1950 to 1999?

    _____

2. How does that relate to what happened to the income generated by groundfish (which includes cod) from 1989 to 1998?

    _____

3. According to graph B, what happened to the monetary value of shellfish from 1989 to 1998?

    _____

4. How do you think the decline in groundfish contributed to the increased fishing of shellfish?

    _____

5. What do you think might happen to shellfish populations if the amount caught keeps increasing?

    _____

PART B

Government regulations that restrict the amount of fish that can be caught have been put in place to prevent overfishing and allow species' populations to recover.

6. Assume that a new regulation restricting the Atlantic Cod catch was put into effect in 1999. Describe what Graph A might look like if the years 2000–2007 were added to it.

Challenge Activity

PART A   Life Zones of the Oceans

What do ocean plants and animals look like? The examples shown in your textbook are only a few of the hundreds of thousands of species that live in the ocean. The purpose of this exercise is to become more familiar with life in different areas of the ocean.

1. Make a large poster to show more examples of ocean life. On the left side of the poster, make a diagram of the benthic environment. Label each zone of the benthic environment. For each, draw at least two life forms that live in the zone. They do not have to be to scale, but be sure to write their actual sizes next to their pictures. Label each creature with its scientific name and its common name. On your poster, include labels for the continental shelf and continental slope.

2. On the right side of the poster, make a diagram of the pelagic environment. Label each zone of this environment and draw pictures of living things in each, as you did for the benthic environment.

3. Are the plants and animals you have drawn threatened by overfishing, pollution, or other human-made or natural dangers? If a plant or animal is in danger, place a star next to its name. On the lines provided, explain what is harming the plant or animal species. In clear sentences, describe any efforts that humans are making to help.

_____

_____

_____

_____

_____

_____

_____

_____

_____

_____

_____

PART B   **Life at Hydrothermal Vents**

Life thrives around hydrothermal vents despite the dark, high pressure, and extreme temperatures. In the past 30 years, more than 300 new species have been identified at hydrothermal vents. Choose one of these species to research. What does it look like? What is known about its life? How does it get food, and what does it eat? Write your findings in a well-organized essay. Include a description of the chemicals it is exposed to from the vent as well as the temperature and pH of the water in which it lives.

Earth's Natural Resources

Key Concept Review

PART A Classify

Classify each term or phrase below by writing it in the appropriate box.

geothermal energy	biomass fuel	natural gas	peat
coal	wood	wind energy	petroleum
nuclear energy	fossil fuel	photovoltaic cell	hydroelectric power
solar energy			

Conventional Energy Resources

Alternative Energy Resources

PART B Comprehension

Read each of the questions below and answer them on the lines provided.
Use a separate sheet of paper if necessary.

1. What are renewable and nonrenewable natural resources?

2. Why will it become necessary to switch from fossil fuels to alternative
    resources for our energy needs?

3. Where do alternative energy resources usually come from?

4. Can alternative energy resources sometimes have a negative impact
    on the environment? Explain.

SCIENCE EXTENSION

Global warming has been shown to cause a variety of negative changes to
Earth's environment. Burning fossil fuels is a large contributor to global warming.
Write a letter to your town or city government representative describing how
your community might switch from using fossil fuels to using alternative sources
of energy, and thus decrease your "carbon footprint" on the environment.

Vocabulary Review

PART A

Complete the following sentences using the correct term from the list. Some words might not be used and some may be used more than once.

biomass fuels	natural gas	petroleum
coal	nonrenewable resources	renewable resources
fossil fuels	peat	sustainable yield

1. Examples of _____ include trees, plants, water, air, and other living things that can be used and replaced over a relatively short period of time. A _____ is a technique used to make sure that a resource is replaced at the same rate at which it is used.

2. _____ form from the remains of once-living organisms over millions of years. Because they take a long time to form, they are _____. One type is _____, a natural or crude oil found underground or along beaches or other areas where it oozes into pits or creeks.

3. _____ come from living things. They are burned directly or converted into gas and alcohol fuels. One type is _____, a light, spongy material harvested from bogs.

PART B

Complete the diagram on solar energy.

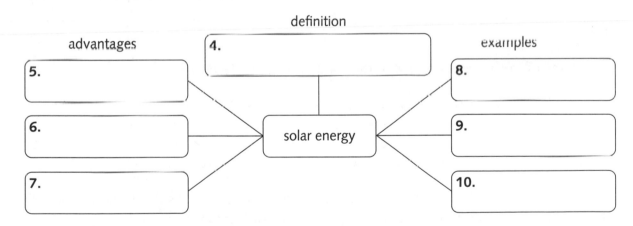

SCIENCE EXTENSION

Write three sentences that use new vocabulary words from the chapter. Leave blanks for the words. Exchange sentences with a partner and fill in the blanks. If an answer is incorrect, give clues, one at a time, until the correct word is chosen.

Graphic Organizer

PART A

Place a check in the column that identifies whether the energy description is a renewable resource, nonrenewable resource, and/or an unlimited resource.

Energy Description	Type of Resource		
	Renewable	Nonrenewable	Unlimited
1. Panels absorb energy, which is stored or pumped through a house and used to heat the house or water.			
2. Natural gas is used to generate electricity and heat buildings. It is used for cooking and to power cars.			
3. Trees are chopped down, and the wood is used for heating and cooking.			
4. Wind turns the blades of turbines, and the energy of the movement of the blades is used to produce electricity.			
5. Petroleum is refined to make jet fuel, gasoline for cars, fuel oil for home heaters, and other fuels such as kerosene and propane.			
6. Methane gas produced in landfills is collected in wells, compressed, and piped to production plants, where it is used to produce electricity.			

PART B

Write the name of the energy resource in the blank next to its description.

_____ **7.** It is the most abundant solid fossil fuel. Over 90 percent of it is used to generate electricity in the United States.

_____ **8.** Ocean waves, waterfalls, and dams are used to generate electricity.

_____ **9.** It is the cleanest-burning fossil fuel. Cars and buses that use it do not pollute the air as much as vehicles that run on gasoline.

_____ **10.** It is one type of biomass fuel that is harvested, dried, and then used to heat homes.

_____ **11.** Power plants use steam released from Earth's crust to produce electricity.

SCIENCE EXTENSION

Write a one-minute radio ad on the importance of energy conservation. Then list three things listeners can do to conserve energy.

Reading Comprehension

PART A K-W-L-H Chart

Natural resources, renewable and nonrenewable, are a hot topic in today's world.
As you read through Lessons 19.1 and 19.2, create a K-W-L-H chart in your Science
Notebook on natural resources. In the column labeled *K,* write what you know about
natural resources. In the column labeled *W,* write what you want to learn about them.
As you identify the information you want to find out about natural resources, write it
in the *L* column. Finally, in the *H* column, write how you can learn more about
natural resources.

PART B Compare and Contrast

Compare and contrast each of the following pairs of terms. Each pair includes two
types of alternative energy resources. If you need to, read Lesson 19.3 again.

1. *passive solar heating & active solar heating* _____

    _____

    _____

2. *wind energy & hydroelectric power* _____

    _____

    _____

3. *geothermal energy & nuclear energy* _____

    _____

    _____

SCIENCE EXTENSION

Conservation

The Konkley family recently made efforts to change their use of renewable and
nonrenewable resources. Their son, Jonathan, made a list of the things they have done
so far. On a separate sheet of paper, identify each conservation choice and how it will
benefit our renewable and nonrenewable resources.

1. Jonathan's father turns the faucet on only to rinse his mouth and his brush when he brushes
    his teeth.

2. Jonathan's grandfather starts collecting aluminum cans to recycle on his daily walk.

3. Jonathan's sister decides to carpool to work.

Math Connection: How Much Sunlight Does It Take to Power a School?

PART A

The Sun is the greatest source of energy on Earth. The amount of solar radiation reaching Earth's surface every year is greater than the amount of energy the world uses in fossil fuels every year. The challenge is to efficiently and economically capture it and convert it into heat and electricity. Right now, solar photovoltaic (pv) panels can only convert 15% of sunlight into electricity.

Suppose a school wants to use solar panels to provide its electricity. Students are asked to help by measuring

a. the average amount of solar radiation each square meter of the roof receives.

b. the total area of the roof where the panels will go.

c. the amount of electricity the school uses.

1. How will the students figure out how much solar radiation the whole roof receives?

   _____

2. How will students figure out how much electricity the pv panels can provide at 15% efficiency?

   _____

PART B

Suppose the amounts the students measure for a, b, and c above are

   a. 5.5 kWH/m²/day (kilowatt-hours per square meter per day)

   b. 210 square meters

   c. 425 kWH per day

Calculate the answers to the following questions. Record your answers on a separate sheet of paper.

3. How much solar radiation does the whole roof receive per day?

4. How much electricity per day can the pv panels provide at 15% electricity?

5. Would the pv panels be able to provide the school with enough electricity? Explain.

Challenge Activity

PART A   Natural Resources In Your Backyard

Every state has different natural resources. Think about the area where you live. Does the land around you have crops or forests? What fuel does the nearest power plant use? Does anyone you know work for a mining company, fishing company, or farm?

Work in groups and conduct research to find out about the natural resources in your home state. Create a large map of your state that illustrates where these natural resources (freshwater, forests, farmland, minerals, coal, natural gas, petroleum) can be found. Mark on the map whether each resource is renewable or nonrenewable.

On the back of your map, write a few sentences explaining how obtaining natural resources has changed over time. For example, are there any mines or forestry operations that have shut down in the last 50 years? Have new ones opened? Share the map with your class when you are finished.

PART B Alternative Energy Resources

Since fossil fuels are nonrenewable and harm the environment, there is a lot of interest in alternative energy resources. Those discussed in Chapter 19 are the most common. Could energy for making electricity or heating buildings also come from other sources?

Develop your own idea for alternative energy, or expand on an idea that you find through research. All new technology starts with an idea, even an idea that might at first seem odd, so be creative. Your alternative energy source could produce enough power to light a home or run a car, or it could give a smaller amount of power (enough to run a few lightbulbs, for example).

Remember that electricity is generated using the energy from motion. Is there some sort of movement that you could use as an energy source? Also remember that carbon and hydrogen in fossil fuels make them good energy sources. Can you think of another source of carbon or hydrogen?

Prepare a class presentation to describe your idea. Include information about whether the energy source is renewable and how the energy would be captured.

SCIENCE EXTENSION

Reduce, Reuse, Recycle

People who want to produce less garbage practice the 3 Rs: reduce, reuse, and recycle. These actions can help to make sure that renewable resources are not used faster than they are naturally formed. They can also increase the time that nonrenewable resources are available. Choose one of these natural resources: freshwater, living things, metals and gemstones, or one of the conventional energy resources. Write an essay about how the 3 Rs relate to this resource. Think of one way people might reduce their use. Is it possible to reuse or recycle? Why or why not? Which of the 3 Rs do you feel will make the biggest difference in conserving this natural resource?

Key Concept Review

PART A Vocabulary

Answer each question below using the correct term from the list.

reclamation	deforestation	greenhouse effect	point sources
crop rotation	smog	acid precipitation	nonpoint sources
monoculture	ozone		

1. _____ is the replanting of vegetation on mined land and the restoration of the land to its original shape.

2. In _____, only one type of crop is grown in a particular area.

3. _____ is a type of air pollution.

4. _____ has a pH less than 5, damages forest soil by removing some essential nutrients, weakens trees, and hastens the decay of city buildings.

5. _____ of pollution generate pollution from widespread sources and locations.

PART B Comprehension

Answer the following questions about the impact humans have on Earth's resources. Use an additional sheet of paper if necessary.

6. Why does surface mining have negative effects on the environment?

_____

7. How does crop rotation help soil?

_____

8. How is clear-cutting of forests damaging to the environment?

_____

9. How does air pollution affect the ozone layer?

_____

SCIENCE EXTENSION

One of the most precious resources on our planet is freshwater. Write a plan showing how you can help prevent pollution of freshwater resources and how you can conserve the amount of water we have.

Vocabulary Review

PART A

Write the correct term next to its definition, using a term from the list. Some terms will not be used.

acid precipitation   groundwater   particulate matter

deforestation   mining   reclamation

global warming   monoculture   smog

greenhouse effect   ozone

_____ **1.** a type of air pollution caused by burning fuels such as wood, coal, or gasoline

_____ **2.** the removal of trees from a large area

_____ **3.** the natural heating of Earth's surface caused by certain gases in the atmosphere

_____ **4.** forms by a chemical reaction that combines oxygen gas with a free oxygen atom

_____ **5.** the process of removing mineral resources from Earth's crust

_____ **6.** a solid particle of material, such as ash, dust, or pollen, which irritates eyes, noses, and throats and can make breathing difficult

PART B

Complete the diagram. Use a separate sheet of paper if necessary.

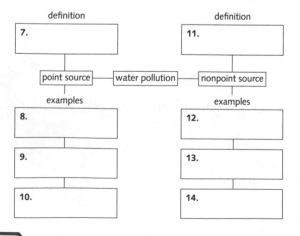

SCIENCE EXTENSION

Write a short story from the viewpoint of a journalist living in 2025. The journalist is touring the country to gather data for a report on the environment. The story should describe the environment and use at least six new terms from the chapter.

Graphic Organizer

PART A

Use these words or phrases to fill in the boxes of the diagram: *acid precipitation, agriculture and forestry, global warming, land, mining, nonpoint source, point source, thinning of the ozone layer, urban development,* and *water.*

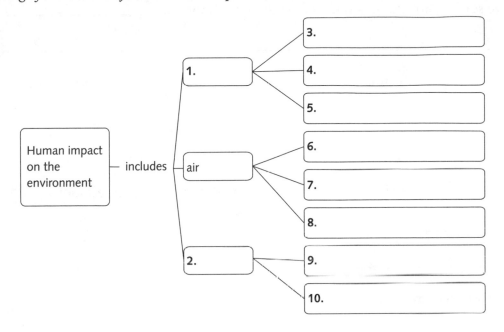

PART B

Place the letter of the description in the correct box of the diagram in Part A.

a. major cause: burning of fossil fuels, which increases levels of carbon dioxide

b. destroys wildlife habitats: clearing of forests and wetlands for construction

c. common source: the discharge of untreated sewage into natural waters

d. monoculture: encourages use of pesticides and fertilizer, which can pollute groundwater, streams, and the water supply

e. major cause: emissions from automobile exhaust and coal-burning power plants

f. sources: runoff from parking lots, faulty septic tanks, pet wastes, road dirt, and grit

g. planting vegetation, part of the process of reclamation, helps repair damage

h. major cause: CFCs, used in refrigerators, aerosol cans, and air conditioners

SCIENCE EXTENSION

Describe an environmental issue in your community that affects the land, water, or air. Locate the source of the issue on a map and the area that is affected. List any activities taken to fix the issue or prevent it from happening again. Include ongoing efforts and things members of the community can do to help fix or prevent the problem.

Reading Comprehension

PART A | **Comprehension**

Lesson 20.1 discusses some ways deforestation adds to global warming. Answer the following questions about what you read.

1. What are some products obtained from cutting down forests? _____

    _____

2. What is clear-cutting? Name three reasons why it is damaging to the environment.

    _____

    _____

3. How are the carbon dioxide levels in our atmosphere affected by deforestation?

    _____

    _____

4. What can we all do to reduce the amount of deforestation? _____

    _____

5. What can the companies who are cutting down forests do to reduce the damaging
    effect of removing trees? _____

    _____

PART B | **Identifying Relationships**

Look at the list of terms below. Using a separate sheet of paper, match a term and a
phrase that seem to go best together. Then, describe the relationship between them.

wells   aerosol spray cans   untreated sewage   point sources

nonpoint sources   soapsuds   groundwater   air pollution

SCIENCE EXTENSION

Would You Buy This Car?

Lori's job is to design a car that is both attractive and environmentally friendly. These
types of cars are sometimes called "green cars." On another sheet of paper, design an
advertisement for a green car of the future. Make a drawing and a list of important
features on your car. Be sure to list any pertinent information such as the source of
energy, type of tires, materials from which the car is made, and at least one thing the
car can do that would actually benefit the environment.

Ecology Connection: Making Cities Greener

PART A

Urban areas have larger human populations; more streets, buildings, and paved areas; and less open space than rural areas. However, people are now protecting, improving, and creating urban "green" spaces such as parks, community gardens, city forests, river corridors, walking and biking paths, and wetlands. These green spaces have many environmental benefits. They improve air quality, reduce noise pollution, absorb rainwater, prevent soil erosion, and provide habitats for plants and animals. They also benefit people. What benefits do you think green spaces have for people's health and happiness? In the graphic organizer below, write three possible health benefits of urban green spaces.

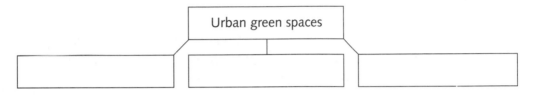

PART B

Imagine that you are an urban planner and you are in charge of improving green spaces in the section of a city shown in the map below. Write in three changes you would make to create or improve green spaces, and indicate where each green space would be on the map. Use a separate sheet of paper if necessary.

4. _____

_____

5. _____

_____

6. _____

_____

SCIENCE EXTENSION

Urban Biodiversity

Biodiversity requires that a large number of different species of plants and animals populate an area. Generally, the more species of plants that live in an area, the more species of animals that will live there also. Write a paragraph in your Science Notebook explaining how green spaces can improve biodiversity in a city.

Challenge Activity

PART A **What Happens to Things That Are Thrown Away?**

1. Everyone places items into the garbage every day. Depending on where you live, the garbage may be picked up daily or weekly. Where is this garbage taken?

Find out more about what happens to your garbage. Start by finding the name of the private company or city department that collects the trash. Use the Internet, write a letter, or call your trash provider to find out where the garbage is taken. Is it a place that people can bring garbage themselves? Is it located near homes or wildlife habitats? Get more information about what things are done by the operators of this landfill or solid waste center to protect the environment. Write your findings in a well-formed paragraph in your Science Notebook.

2. There are several city and state rules about what can and cannot be placed into household garbage. For example, some things like oil paints, electronics, or old tires might not be allowed in the regular trash.

Find out from your city or trash collector what items or materials should not be put into the garbage. Make a list of these items. For at least two of these items, write a sentence describing why you think they are not allowed. Then, find out how you would properly dispose of them. Does your city have a special place to take them? Must you hire a professional to take these items? Finally, research whether there is another item that could be used for the same purpose.

PART B Water Quality In the Nation's Waterways

A state's lakes, rivers, and bays are checked from time to time for pollution, invasive plants or animals, and other things that lower the quality of the water. This information is reported to the Environmental Protection Agency. Depending on the condition of the water, the lakes and rivers may be given a grade such as "good" or "impaired" (harmed or damaged).

3. Choose a body of water within the county you live in. Find the most recent information about its water quality. Is the water in good condition or does it contain pollution? If it is polluted, where did the pollution come from? Write your findings in six to ten well-formed sentences on the lines provided.

_____

_____

_____

_____

_____

_____

_____

_____

_____

_____

_____

_____

_____

_____

Key Concept Review

PART A Outlining

As you read, fill in the outline of the chapter below using the main headings and subheadings of each lesson.

21.1: _____ D. _____

    A. _____ E. _____

    B. _____ F. _____

    C. _____ 21.3: _____

    D. _____   A. _____

21.2: _____   B. _____

    A. _____   C. _____

    B. _____   D. _____

    C. _____

PART B Vocabulary

Circle the word that best completes each sentence below.

1. (Astronomy, Cosmology, Meteorology) is the study of the universe, how it formed, and its future.

2. An object that orbits another is called a (moon, star, satellite).

3. The fact that the Moon rotates exactly one time each time it travels around Earth is called (perigee, synchronous rotation, apogee).

4. The closest point to Earth in the Moon's orbit is called (perigee, synchronous rotation, apogee).

5. (Refraction, Reflection, Electromagnetic radiation) is made up of electric and magnetic disturbances that travel through space as waves.

SCIENCE EXTENSION

The electromagnetic spectrum is a range of wavelengths of light, from the shortest to the longest. Some of these types of light are visible, while others are not. Draw an electromagnetic spectrum, including the range of visible light, and label each type of radiation on the spectrum, from short to long. Use this chapter, the Internet, and the library to help you label your diagram. Then write a paragraph briefly describing each of the types of radiation on the spectrum.

Vocabulary Review

PART A

Decide whether each statement is true or false. If a statement is true, write *true* in the blank. If the statement is false, replace the underlined term with the letter of the term that makes it true.

a. apogee
d. wavelength
g. satellite

b. cosmology
e. penumbra
h. umbra

c. ecliptic
f. perigee
i. electromagnetic radiation

_____ 1. The Moon experiences <u>synchronous rotation</u>, which means that it rotates exactly one time each time it travels around Earth.

_____ 2. The <u>electromagnetic spectrum</u> is made up of electric and magnetic disturbances that travel in waves.

_____ 3. <u>Astronomy</u> is the study of the universe, how it formed, and its future.

_____ 4. At <u>apogee</u>, the Moon is as close as 356,000 km to Earth.

_____ 5. The Moon appears 30 percent larger at <u>perigee</u> than at apogee to viewers on Earth.

_____ 6. Earth's orbit, viewed from the side, makes a plane called the <u>penumbra</u>.

PART B

The diagram below shows Earth's tilt and its orbital rotation around the Sun. Label and define the following in the diagram: summer solstice, winter solstice, autumnal equinox, and vernal equinox.

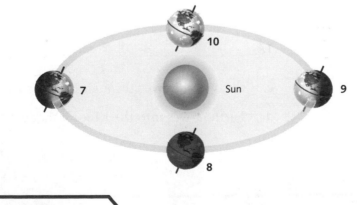

SCIENCE EXTENSION

Use a Venn diagram to compare and contrast refracting telescopes and reflecting telescopes.

Interpreting Diagrams

PART A

Identify the lunar phases in the diagram below. Shade the part of the Moon that is not visible during each phase. Then complete the statements that follow the diagram.

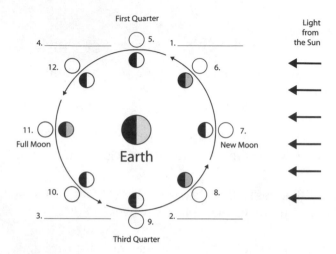

13. The Moon goes through all of its phases every _____.

14. When Earth is between the Sun and the Moon, the viewer sees a _____.

15. During waxing phases, the amount of reflected sunlight seen on Earth _____.

16. During waning phases, the amount of reflected sunlight seen on Earth _____.

PART B

Write the correct letters under the diagrams below.

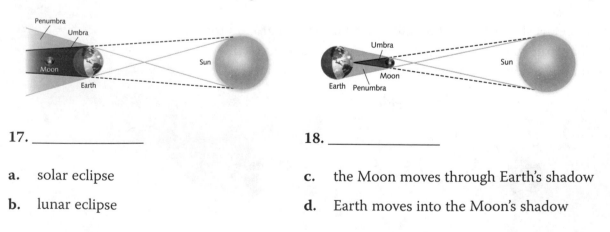

17. _____   18. _____

a. solar eclipse   c. the Moon moves through Earth's shadow

b. lunar eclipse   d. Earth moves into the Moon's shadow

SCIENCE EXTENSION

Research the types of artificial satellites orbiting Earth. Then write a paragraph on the purpose and benefits of one of the types of satellites and what the impact would be if we could no longer communicate with any satellites of that type.

Reading Comprehension

PART A **Sounds Like It**

The following pairs of words differ in spelling but sound very similar when spoken. On a separate sheet of paper, write each pair of words. Four of the pairs have only one term used in Chapter 21. Circle that term and write a definition for it in your own words, based on how it is used in this chapter. There is one pair in which both terms are used in Chapter 21. Define both of those terms.

1. cosmology, cosmetology

2. ecliptic, elliptic

3. pedigree, perigee

4. synchronize, synchronous

5. gamma, grandma

PART B **Vocabulary Flashcards**

Lesson 21.1 introduces many new terms describing solstices and equinoxes. Create a flashcard for each vocabulary term in Lesson 21.1. On one side, write the vocabulary term. On the other side, write the definition and at least one interesting fact about that term. To help categorize the different terms, you might choose to use different colors for the terms. Test your ability to memorize the flashcards. Practice alone or with a partner.

SCIENCE EXTENSION

Other Wavelength Uses

Match the waves and rays with their uses. It might be helpful to look at the electromagnetic spectrum in Lesson 21.3.

1. On Earth, these rays are used in CT scans, to sterilize medical equipment, and to treat cancer. These are powerful rays with the highest frequencies and the shortest wavelengths.

    A. infrared waves

2. These rays can be detected by a method known as photographic plates. They are especially useful in the detection of skeletal problems.

    B. radio waves

3. These waves are thermal. We feel this type of wave in the form of heat from sunlight, a fire, or a warm sidewalk.

    C. visible light waves

4. These are waves with the longest wavelengths, some longer than a football field. These waves transmit information through cell phones, TVs, and radios.

    D. X rays

5. These are the only electromagnetic waves we can see. When all of these waves are seen together, they make white light.

    E. gamma rays

Astronomy Connection: Tracking the Sun

PART A

Many ancient cultures learned to use the Sun as a calendar, using its movements to mark the seasons. The diagram below shows the movement of the Sun on three days during the year. Based on where the Sun would be in the sky on these days, label the summer solstice (June 21), the winter solstice (December 21), and the spring equinox (March 21). On the lines below, describe these three days.

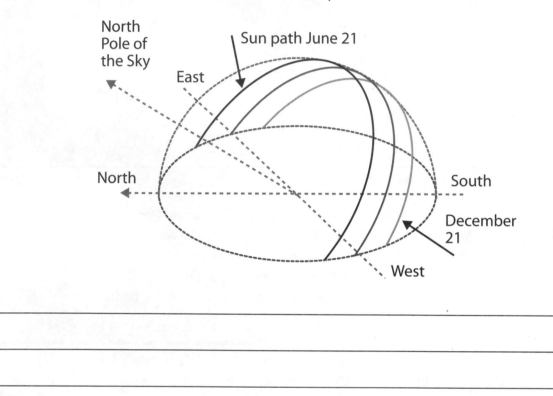

1. _____

2. _____

3. _____

PART B

Many of these ancient cultures built "Sunwheels," or circles of standing stones, to align with the Sun at the solstices and equinoxes. Imagine that you are building a Sunwheel. You want to use large stones to mark the cardinal directions and also where the Sun rises and sets on the summer and winter solstices. On the circle below, label approximately where these stones would be placed using the diagram above as a guide.

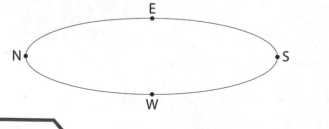

SCIENCE EXTENSION

Casting Shadows

Is your shadow longer at noon on the winter solstice or on the summer solstice? Research the answer to this question. Write and explain your answer in your Science Notebook.

Challenge Activity

PART A   Maria of the Moon

In Latin the word *mare* means *sea*. The smooth plains of the Moon were named *maria* because very early Moon observers thought they might be seas. We now know this is not true. The early names given to the maria of the Moon are still used (for example, Sea of Nectar, or Mare Nectaris).

Do your own research to learn the answers to the questions below. Be sure to use both spellings (*mare* and *maria*) in your search.

1. In which mare did *Apollo 11* land?

   _____

2. Which is the largest mare on the side of the Moon facing Earth?

   _____

3. What is the shape and diameter of this mare?

   _____

   _____

4. What are two maria that were named for people?

   _____

   _____

5. On which side of the Moon are the most maria found?

   _____

6. How much of the Moon's surface is covered by the maria?

   _____

   _____

PART B   **Journey to the Moon**

Sending astronauts to the Moon was a historic achievement that sparked public interest in space programs. During the late 1960s and early 1970s there were six manned spacecraft that landed on the Moon.

7. Do more research about the history of lunar landings. When did a spacecraft carrying astronauts first land on the Moon? What was its name? Who were the first astronauts to walk on the Moon? When was the last time that astronauts visited the Moon? What was the name of this spacecraft? Write your findings in a well-ordered paragraph.

8. If you could have spoken to one of the astronauts after they returned to Earth, what would you want to know about his experience? Imagine that you were a reporter at this time. Prepare a list of ten questions that you would like to ask him.

9. Given the costs and risks, do you think that we should continue to send men and women into space? Or do you feel that their work could be done with unmanned spacecraft? In your Science Notebook, write an opinion piece about the space program that would run in a newspaper. Be sure to provide good arguments to support your idea.

Key Concept Review

PART A Sequencing

Number the following planets in the correct order, starting from the planet closest to the Sun and moving outward. On the second blank, write whether the planet is a terrestrial planet or a gas giant planet.

Mars _____ _____   Saturn _____ _____

Earth _____ _____   Venus _____ _____

Uranus _____ _____   Jupiter _____ _____

Mercury _____ _____   Neptune _____ _____

PART B Comprehension

Read each of the questions about the solar system and answer them on the lines provided.

1. What is a nebula? What body in our solar system formed in a nebula?

    _____

    _____

2. What are planetesimals?

    _____

    _____

3. What is the difference between a meteoroid and a meteorite?

    _____

    _____

4. What force keeps the planets in orbit around the Sun? What force keeps the planets from moving in toward the Sun?

    _____

SCIENCE EXTENSION

Choose one planet other than Earth to explore. Write a paragraph imagining what a day on that planet would be like. How long is one day on the planet? How about one year? What is the atmosphere like? What is the surface like? Use the information from this chapter as well as from other sources to fill in the details about your chosen planet.

Chapter 22

The Solar System

Vocabulary Review

PART A

Match each term in Column B with its description in Column A. Write the letter of the correct term in the space provided.

Column A

1. _____ small bodies made of ice and rock, most of which travel in elliptical orbits around the Sun

2. _____ when a planet is closest to the Sun in its orbit

3. _____ tiny grains of condensed matter that eventually formed planets

4. _____ the tendency of an object at rest to remain at rest and the tendency of an object in motion to stay in motion

5. _____ small, rocky bodies that orbit the Sun

6. _____ hot, condensed material at the center of a nebula

7. _____ the Sun, the planets, and other bodies that travel around it

8. _____ huge clouds of gas and dust from which the solar system formed

9. _____ the time it takes a planet to make one complete revolution around the Sun

10. _____ when a planet is farthest from the Sun in its orbit

Column B

a. aphelion

b. asteroids

c. comets

d. inertia

e. nebula

f. orbital period

g. perihelion

h. planetesimals

i. protostar

j. solar system

PART B

Complete the flow chart by placing the correct word and its definition in each box: meteor, meteorite, and meteoroid.

11. _____ → 12. _____ → 13. _____

SCIENCE EXTENSION

Write two questions for each set of terms that help explain the difference between them: *geocentric* or *heliocentric*, *perihelion* or *aphelion*, *retrograde rotation* or *prograde rotation*, and *meteorite* or *meteoroid*. Exchange questions with a partner and have the partner circle the correct word for each question.

Interpreting Diagrams

PART A

Label the diagram with the names of the planets and their distances from the Sun in astronomical units.

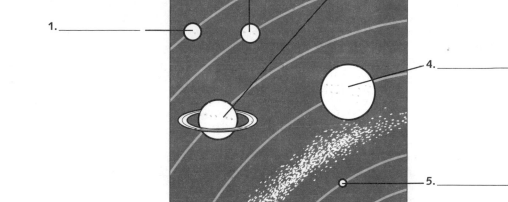

2. _____ 3. _____

1. _____

4. _____

5. _____

6. _____

7. _____

8. _____

Sun

PART B

Place the letter of the description next to the planet or planets in the diagram. Each planet can have more than one letter, and letters can be used more than once.

a. terrestrial planets that have solid, rocky surfaces

b. gaseous planets that do not have a solid surface

c. planet with the shortest day

d. planet with the largest difference between day and night temperatures

e. hottest planet in the solar system

f. A small amount of methane in the atmosphere makes it appear bluish.

g. Its largest moon is Titan.

h. experiences seasons because it is tilted on its axis

i. has belts and zones and a Great Red Spot

j. has ten rings that stand upright and is tilted 90 degrees on its axis

k. has a greenhouse effect

l. Seven major rings extend out almost 300,000 km, but are less than 200 m thick.

SCIENCE EXTENSION

Use a Venn diagram to compare and contrast three terrestrial planets or three gas giants.

Reading Comprehension

PART A **Outlining**

Outlines can help you remember what you read about the solar system. Look at the headings and the subheadings in Lesson 22.1. Complete the outline below. If you need to, read the section again.

Section 22.1	How Was the Solar System Formed?
Heading	**Main Idea**
1. The _____ Nebula	**2.** This is the _____ that formed into our own solar system.
Our Solar System	**3.** It consists of the _____ and the _____. It also includes other bodies that travel around it.
Planet Formation	**4.** The solar nebula _____, and the attraction between particles got stronger. Solid particles called _____ stuck together when they collided, forming the building blocks of the _____.
Asteroids	**5.** They orbit the _____ and are thought to be pieces of _____.
Meteoroid	These are fragments of asteroids.
Meteor	**6.** When a meteorite burns up, it produces streaks of _____, called a _____.
Meteorite	**7.** This is a meteoroid that has entered _____ atmosphere and strikes the _____.
Comets	**8.** These are made up of _____ and _____. They have a _____ and one or more _____.
Meteor Shower	**9.** This is also known as _____ stars.

PART B **Comprehension**

This chapter uses many words or phrases that you might have heard in math class. Sometimes these words are defined. Sometimes you have to use context clues or the dictionary to find out what they mean.

10. In your own words, how do you define *foci*? _____

_____

11. What is an AU unit of measure? _____

SCIENCE EXTENSION

Students used to say the acronym "My Very Educated Mother Just Served Us Nine Pizzas" to learn the order of the planets. Write an explanation of why this no longer works.

Physics Connection: The Force of Gravity

PART A

Objects should fall toward Earth at the same speed unless there are other forces, such as air resistance, acting upon them. In the Explore It! activity on p. 418, you dropped different objects from the same height and compared the rate at which they fell. For each of the pairs listed below, explain which one would fall faster and why, or if they would fall at the same speed.

1. a rock and a paper clip _____

_____

2. a crumpled-up piece of paper and a flat piece of paper _____

_____

3. a hammer and a pencil _____

_____

4. a tennis ball and a feather _____

_____

PART B

The Moon has less mass than Earth, so it has less gravitational force. Gravity on the Moon is one-sixth that of Earth's. There is no air resistance on the Moon because there is no atmosphere. Use this information to answer the following questions:

5. What would happen if you dropped a rock and a paper clip on the Moon? How would it be different from dropping them on Earth? _____

_____

_____

6. What would happen if you dropped a tennis ball and a feather on the Moon? How would it be different from dropping them on Earth? _____

_____

_____

SCIENCE EXTENSION

Remember that what you weigh depends on gravity. If you weigh 150 pounds on Earth, and gravity on the Moon is one-sixth that of Earth's, what would you weigh on the Moon?

Challenge Activity

PART A **Distances Between Planets**

It is hard to imagine how large the solar system is or how great the distance is between the Sun and the planets. A scale model will not even fit indoors. In this exercise you will make an outdoor scale model of the solar system.

Start by finding the average distance, in km and in miles, of each planet from the Sun. The table below has this distance in astronomical units (AU) to the nearest tenth. Use this information to find miles or kilometers. It might be easiest to use the approximate values. Round your answers to the nearest million.

1 astronomical unit = 1.496×10^8 km, or ~150 million km

1 astronomical unit = 9.296×10^7 miles, or ~93 million miles

Planet	Average Distance From the Sun (AU)	Average Distance From the Sun (miles)	Average Distance From the Sun (km)
Mercury	0.39	1.	9.
Venus	0.72	2.	10.
Earth	1.00	3.	11.
Mars	1.52	4.	12.
Jupiter	5.20	5.	13.
Saturn	9.55	6.	14.
Uranus	19.18	7.	15.
Neptune	30.11	8.	16.

Now, imagine that you are going to use a football field for your scale model. The Sun will be on one goal line. You need to find the distance from that goal line to each of the planets. Find a scale that will work for the model, so that all the planets fit on the field. For example, you could try a scale of 1 million miles = 0.1 yards.

17. In this scale, would Neptune fit on the field? _____

If not, try a different scale. When you have chosen a scale you like, write it on the next page. Then use it to find the distance of each planet on the field. Round to the nearest tenth of a yard. Record your answers in the table.

Then, as a class, make your scale model. Have one person stand in for each planet and one person be the Sun. Are the distances between planets what you imagined?

Scale for model: _____

Planet	Distance From Goal Line (yards) Scale: 1 million miles =	Distance From Goal Line (yards) Scale: 1 million km =
Mercury	18.	26.
Venus	19.	27.
Earth	20.	28.
Mars	21.	29.
Jupiter	22.	30.
Saturn	23.	31.
Uranus	24.	32.
Neptune	25.	33.

What if you wanted to put models of the planets, instead of people, into your scale model? Use your scale and the actual diameters of the planets to find the diameters of model planets. Then think of an object to represent the planet. Would an acorn work? a beach ball? the head of a pin? Write your ideas in the table.

Scale for models: _____

Planet	Diameter for Model	Object for Planet Model
Mercury	34.	42.
Venus	35.	43.
Earth	36.	44.
Mars	37.	45.
Jupiter	38.	46.
Saturn	39.	47.
Uranus	40.	48.
Neptune	41.	49.

PART B   Planet Names

A mnemonic device is a tool for remembering things. For example, "She makes Harry eat onions" is a sentence that can help you remember the names of the Great Lakes from west to east: *S*uperior, *M*ichigan, *H*uron, *E*rie, *O*ntario.

Make your own mnemonic device to remember the order of the planets, from closest to the Sun to farthest away. Then, try to find a mnemonic device to remember the sizes of the planets, from largest diameter to smallest diameter or from greatest mass to least mass. Share these with your class.

Key Concept Review

PART A Outlining

As you read, fill in the outline of the chapter below using the main headings and subheadings of each lesson.

23.1: _____

    A. _____

    B. _____

    C. _____

23.2: _____

    A. _____

    B. _____

C. _____

23.3: _____

    A. _____

    B. _____

    C. _____

    D. _____

PART B Vocabulary

Circle the term that best completes each sentence below.

1. The (corona, photosphere, chromosphere) is the outermost layer of the Sun.

2. The Sun and all other stars produce energy through the process of nuclear (fission, radiation, fusion).

3. A star can be classified by the unique pattern of lines in its (continuous spectrum, absorption spectrum, radiation spectrum).

4. The brightness of a star as it appears to observers on Earth is called its (apparent magnitude, absolute magnitude, luminosity).

5. A (red giant, white dwarf, black hole) forms when a supergiant star dies.

SCIENCE EXTENSION

Stars begin to form in clouds of gas and dust called nebulae. They go through life cycles that vary according to the size of the star formed. Using the information in this chapter and other sources, write a brief biography of the Sun up to its current state. Then predict what the rest of its life cycle will be like.

Vocabulary Review

PART A

Match the following definitions to the correct word in the list below. Write the letter of the definition in the blank next to the word.

1. _____ aurora   4. _____ fusion   7. _____ solar flare

2. _____ black hole   5. _____ neutron star   8. _____ solar wind

3. _____ photosphere   6. _____ parallax   9. _____ supernova

a. the process by which lightweight nuclei are combined into heavier nuclei, such as hydrogen to helium, which powers the Sun

b. this forms when massive stars collapse on themselves and form a single point in space

c. huge explosion in which the entire outer portion of a star is blown off

d. made up of gas and charged solar particles that flow outward from the corona

e. the apparent change in a star's position due to the movement of the observer

f. extremely dense stars that are 1.5 to 4 times bigger than the Sun

g. violent eruptions of particles and radiation from the Sun's surface

h. light display that occurs when charged particles from the Sun collide with gases from Earth's upper atmosphere

i. the lowest layer of the Sun's atmosphere

PART B

Label the diagram with the following terms: *luminosity, main sequence, red giant, supergiant,* and *white dwarf.*

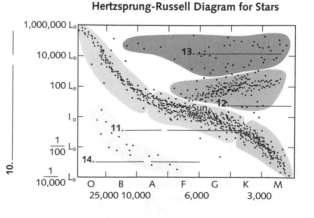

Hertzsprung-Russell Diagram for Stars

SCIENCE EXTENSION

Write a dialogue in which two students discuss the meanings of these terms: *absolute magnitude, apparent magnitude,* and *luminosity.*

Interpreting Diagrams

PART A

Label the diagram using the following terms: *chromosphere, convective zone, core, corona, photosphere, radiative zone,* and *sunspot.*

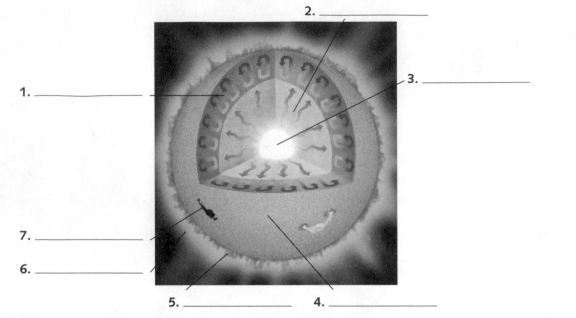

2. _____

1. _____

3. _____

7. _____

6. _____

5. _____   4. _____

PART B

Match the words in the diagram to the descriptions below. Write the words on the lines.

8. zone closest to the core: energy transferred by gas particles _____

9. outermost layer of the Sun's atmosphere: ranges from 1–2 million K _____

10. more helium in this layer of the Sun's atmosphere gives it a red color _____

11. zone in which energy is carried through convection currents to the
Sun's surface _____

12. interior region: the place where fusion takes place; temperature is about
15 million K _____

13. this layer appears as the visible surface of the Sun and is about 5,800 K _____

14. dark, cooler patch on the surface of the photosphere _____

SCIENCE EXTENSION

Draw a diagram in your Science Notebook that shows the life cycles of a medium-sized star and of a massive star. Then write a short paragraph that compares and contrasts the life cycles of the stars.

Reading Comprehension

PART A **Complete the Sentences**

In each of the following sentences, choose a word from the word box to correctly complete the sentence. Use the bolded terms to help you, or read the chapter again.

| red giant | white dwarf | parallax | protostar |
| nebula | fusion | corona | supernova |

1. A _____ **explosion** produces heavy elements such as silver, gold, and lead and can light up the sky for days.

2. Stars do not move, but when they **appear to change** position in the sky due to the movement of the observer, we call this _____.

3. A _____ is a **tiny** dense star with its matter packed tightly together.

4. A _____ is the **hot glowing center** of condensed dust and gas.

5. The process of **producing energy** known as _____ is the source of the Sun's power.

6. When a medium-sized star gets older, the star's core begins to shrink, while its outer shell expands, cools, and turns **red;** then it becomes a _____.

7. All stars begin as a **cloud** of gas and dust called a _____.

8. The _____ is the **outermost layer** of the Sun's atmosphere.

PART B **Compare and Contrast**

Use a separate sheet of paper to describe in your own words, how each pair of terms is similar and different.

9. *apparent magnitude, absolute magnitude*:

10. *solar flares, solar winds*:

11. *neutron star, black hole*:

SCIENCE EXTENSION

Your friend recently purchased a telescope and invited you over to look at the stars. While you are looking at the night sky, he tells you about a question that has been puzzling him. "If all stars are basically made up of helium and hydrogen, why are some of them blue, while others are yellow or red?" Write an explanation that answers your friend's question.

Literature Connection: The Constellations

PART A

Thousands of years ago, ancient people created stories to explain the star patterns they saw in the night sky. Often these patterns, or constellations, were connected with stories or myths. The constellations were named after animals or characters that they resembled, and stories were created around them. Most of the constellation names that we now use—and the stories about them—come from ancient Greece or Rome. Five constellations are shown below. Use their shapes to match them with the correct name.

Orion—The Hunter   Leo—The Lion   Cygnus—The Swan

Taurus—The Bull   Cassiopeia—The Queen
                                  (her throne)

1. _____   2. _____   3. _____

4. _____   5. _____

PART B

Different cultures have recognized different patterns in the sky. Use your library and the Internet to research a constellation from Greek, Roman, Native American, Chinese, or African mythology. Choose a constellation that interests you and read about its mythology. In your Science Notebook, draw the constellation and summarize one of the myths about it.

SCIENCE EXTENSION

The constellation Taurus contains The Crab Nebula, the remnants of a supernova that was observed in A.D. 1054. It was recorded by Chinese and Arab astronomers. It was reportedly so bright that it was observable during the day for 23 days. Inside the nebula is a pulsar that regularly emits beams of radiation. What size star was it before it exploded in a supernova? What could eventually form from this nebula?

Challenge Activity

PART A   Studying the Sun

1. Imagine that you are a scientist who studies the Sun. In your Science Notebook, write a letter to your family and friends that describes your research, where you work, and what types of instruments you use. For example, do you use telescopes or is most of your work computer modeling? Which part of the Sun do you study? Include drawings and diagrams in your letter.

PART B   Stars

Some well-known stars are listed below. Research these stars and use the information to match the star to its description.

2. Sirius A _____

3. Rigel _____

4. Betelgeuse _____

5. Antares _____

6. Arcturus _____

7. Pollux _____

8. Polaris _____

9. Proxima Centauri _____

a. This star is the brightest star seen in the night sky.

b. This is a supergiant in the constellation Ursa Minor.

c. This tiny star is the Sun's nearest neighbor.

d. This giant star is about 35 million light years away from our solar system. Its apparent magnitude is approximately 0, and it appears orange in color.

e. This star is about 34 million light years away from our solar system. It has an apparent magnitude of around 1.1.

f. This supergiant is also called Alpha Scorpii and is in the constellation Scorpius. It has variable brightness.

g. This supergiant is the brightest star in the constellation Orion. Its apparent magnitude is 0.12.

h. This star, also known as Alpha Orionis, is part of the constellation Orion. Its image was the first image of a star, other than the Sun, taken by the Hubble telescope.

10. Choose two different-sized stars from the list. Make a poster describing the life cycle of these stars. Start with the birth of the star and continue on. At what stage is each star now? What is likely to happen to the stars in the future? Include a time line of each star's life. Use the space below for notes.

_____

_____

_____

_____

_____

_____

_____

_____

_____

_____

_____

_____

_____

_____

_____

_____

_____

_____

_____

_____

_____

_____

Key Concept Review

PART A Vocabulary

Answer each question below using the correct term from the box. You will not use all
of the terms.

galaxy	irregular galaxy	quasars	big bang theory
spiral galaxy	globular clusters	universe	cosmic background radiation

1. The _____ states that the universe began from a tiny point
   and has continually increased in size.

2. _____, faraway star-like objects, are some of the brightest
   objects in the universe.

3. _____ are groups of older stars.

4. A(n) _____ is a large group of stars, planets, and other space
   objects that does not have a normal, uniform, or symmetrical shape.

5. _____ is low-level radiation from space that creates noise
   on radio antennae.

PART B Comprehension

Read each of the questions about galaxies and the universe and answer them
on the lines provided. Use a separate sheet of paper.

6. Does the existence of cosmic background radiation support or go against
   the big bang theory? Explain.

7. What is the estimated age of the universe?

8. Why are scientists so interested in quasars?

9. How does the redshift that occurs with light from distant galaxies show that
   the universe is expanding?

SCIENCE EXTENSION

Galaxies form in many shapes and sizes. Our own galaxy, the Milky Way, is a spiral
galaxy. Research another galaxy in the universe. Compare and contrast it to the Milky
Way in terms of its shape, its estimated age, and its distance from Earth.

Vocabulary Review

PART A

Complete the sentences below using terms from the following list: *cosmic background radiation, elliptical galaxy, galaxy, globular clusters, irregular galaxy, open clusters, quasar,* and *universe.*

1. Groups of older stars packed tightly into a roughly spherical shape are _____. _____ are smaller and made up of younger stars.

2. A(n) _____ contains only old stars and has a bright center.

3. A _____, one of the brightest objects in the universe, looks like a star but emits radio waves and types of light waves that stars do not emit.

4. Everything that exists throughout space is contained in the _____.

PART B

Complete the diagram on the big bang theory.

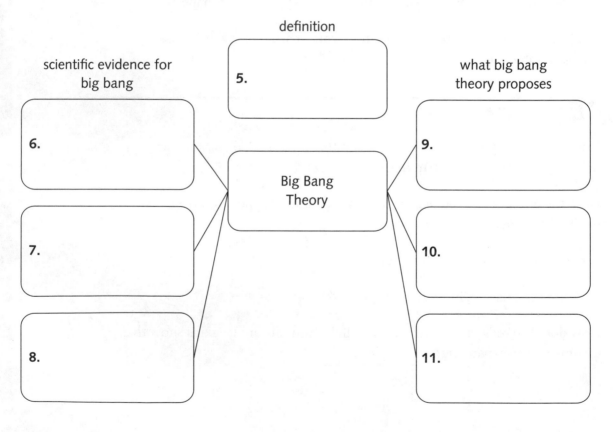

definition

scientific evidence for big bang

what big bang theory proposes

5.

6.

7.

8.

Big Bang Theory

9.

10.

11.

SCIENCE EXTENSION

Write two clues each for two of the following terms: *spiral galaxy, elliptical galaxy, irregular galaxy, globular clusters, open clusters,* and *quasar.* Exchange clues with a partner and have your partner identify the correct term.

Interpreting Diagrams

PART A

Identify each type of galaxy shown below.

1. _____   2. _____   3. _____

PART B

In the space next to each description, write *E* for elliptical galaxy, *I* for irregular galaxy, and *S* for spiral galaxy.

_____ 4. has a flat, disk-like shape

_____ 5. generally the youngest of the galaxies

_____ 6. has tightly packed groups of stars that contain little dust or gas

_____ 7. Most galaxies are this type.

_____ 8. The Milky Way galaxy is this type.

_____ 9. Virgo A is this type of galaxy.

_____ 10. A central bulge contains older stars, and arms contain younger stars, dust, and gases.

_____ 11. The Antennae Galaxies are this type.

_____ 12. has a bright center and contains only old stars

Circle the word that correctly completes the statement.

13. Currently, the expansion rate of the universe is (decreasing, increasing).

14. The twin paradox, based on the special theory of relativity, states that if you travel near the speed of light to a distant star and then return to Earth, your twin will be (younger, older) than you.

15. Based on its expansion rate and cosmic radiation levels, the age of the universe is estimated to be (13.7 billion, 18 billion) years old.

SCIENCE EXTENSION

Research a galaxy, such as the Milky Way or Andromeda. Draw sketches of the galaxy and label it with various facts, such as the location and names of stars in the galaxy, its size, its distance from Earth or our galaxy, the type of galaxy, and so on.

Reading Comprehension

PART A Vocabulary Flashcards

Create a flashcard for each vocabulary term in Chapter 24. On one side, write the vocabulary term. On the other side, write the definition and at least one interesting fact about that term. To help categorize the different terms, use a different color pen for each lesson's terms. Test your ability to memorize all the flashcards. Practice alone or with a partner.

PART B True or False

If the statement is true, write "true." If it is false, change the underlined word or words to make the statement true.

1. The Milky Way galaxy is part of a small group of galaxies called the <u>Local Group</u>. _____

2. Edwin Hubble classified galaxies by their <u>color</u>. _____

3. <u>Younger</u> stars give off a bluish color because they are hotter. _____

4. Quasars are <u>very bright stars</u> that are about the size of an average-sized solar system. _____

5. <u>Spiral</u> galaxies have very bright centers and very little dust and gas. _____

SCIENCE EXTENSION

Model Madness

A local museum has models of all the spacecraft used or soon to be used by NASA. One day, the museum had a full house of young children. Many of the labels of the names on the models got removed. Thankfully, the description of each model remained in place. Help the museum staff match the names with the models. Use the list of names and the *End of Unit 9 Case Studies* to help you.

Mariner 9	Mars Science Laboratory	Phoenix
Stardust	Saturn V	Orion

1. This is a replica of a probe that passed through a comet's tail, trapping tiny particles of comet gas and dust. _____

2. This is a model of what NASA will send to Mars in 2010. Its purpose will be to look for signs of life past or present. _____

3. Sitting on top of the Ares I, this six-person vehicle will one day carry astronauts to an international space station. _____

4. This is a model of the spacecraft that will be the first to study one of Mars's poles. _____

Technology Connection: Getting a Better View of the Universe

PART A

NASA is building a new space telescope called the James Webb Space Telescope (JWST) to replace the Hubble Space Telescope. It will be stationed 1.5 million km from Earth. It has many new features that will enable it to observe objects in the universe that are farther away and fainter than anything that has yet been observed.

Use the illustration and facts about the JWST to answer the questions that follow. Use a separate sheet of paper if necessary.

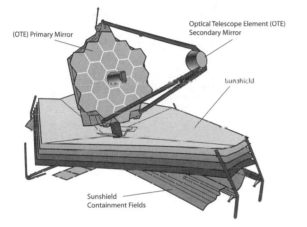

(OTE) Primary Mirror

Optical Telescope Element (OTE) Secondary Mirror

sunshield

Sunshield Containment Fields

James Webb Space Telescope Features

- captures infrared light
- stationed far from Earth and closer to other objects in space
- 6.5-meter mirror for collecting infrared light
- tennis court-sized sunshield to block light from the Sun, Earth, and the Moon
- microshutters to block out nearby light and see further objects better
- telescope that can penetrate clouds of interstellar dust

1. How will the JWST be equipped to search for early stars, galaxies, and other objects formed after the Big Bang?

   _____

2. Why do you think that blocking out nearby light can better enable the telescope to see distant objects?

   _____

3. How does penetrating interstellar dust clouds help the telescope to observe the formation of stars and planetary systems?

   _____

PART B

Name three objects that astronomers might study with the JWST in order to learn about the formation of the universe, stars, and planetary systems.

4. _____   5. _____   6. _____

Challenge Activity

PART A Crab Nebula

The Chinese observed the explosion of the supernova that formed the Crab Nebula almost 1,000 years ago, in A.D. 1054. When did the explosion actually occur? Remember that it takes time for light to travel from distant sources to Earth.

1. What is the speed of light?

    _____

2. The Crab Nebula is approximately 2 kiloparsecs away from Earth. What is a parsec? How many light-years are in one parsec?

    _____

3. What is a kiloparsec? How many light-years are in a kiloparsec?

    _____

4. What is the meaning of a light-year?

    _____

5. Using this information, how would you determine how long ago, in Earth years, the supernova exploded?

    _____

    _____

6. Is there a different series of steps you could take to find or check the answer using the speed of light?

    _____

    _____

7. When did the supernova that formed the Crab Nebula explode? Figure this out in two different ways to check your answer. If you use rounding, remember that the answer will be approximate.

    _____

    _____

PART B **Quasars**

The name quasar comes from "quasi-stellar," since quasars can look like stars. However, quasars give off different types of radiation.

8. Think about radiation and quasars. Why were quasars not discovered until after the development of radio telescopes in the 1940s?

_____

9. Quasar 3C 273 is the brightest quasar in the visible sky. Do your own research to learn how this quasar got its name.

_____

_____

10. Do more research about a quasar other than 3C 273. What is the name of this quasar? How far away is it from Earth in light-years? Is it considered to be part of a constellation? Write your findings in a well-ordered paragraph in your Science Notebook. If you find a picture of the quasar, include it or make a sketch.